PAARA MI HERMANA
CHRISTINA QUE
CRESCA EN RUYNA
LUZ
LETERRNA

Valdeson Borges

10 / 04 / 13

Other books by Michael Edward Owens

The Way of Truth Eternal – Book I

Babaji – the Beginning Has No End

Ekere Tere – City of Light

Discovery of Self – Answers to Questions of the God Seeker

Paramitas – The Gathering of Many Rivers

Guardians of the Gates of Heaven

Principles – Foundations of the Light and Sound

Spiritual Comfort – Language of the Heart

Spiritual Comfort

Michael Edward Owens

OPEN HEART BOOKS

~Introduction~

The pathway home to the Heart of Sugmad (God) has been traveled by countless Souls, and now you, too, make this sublime journey back to the beginning that has no end.

Along the way, you will be provided with many and varied resources to aid you in your progress. "Spiritual Comfort" is one such resource that has been brought to you through Grace as one of the innumerable blessings offered by The Living Sehaji Master, Sri Michael Owens, who serves as the Inner Master, Dan Rin.

As a collection of spiritual exercises, poems, and prayers compiled from his writings and talks from 2005-2008, this book will serve as a bright beacon upon the path and a source of immeasurable insight and inspiration.

Most importantly, it will serve as a practical resource for your having immediate access to the keys to the Inner Worlds of beingness that are awaiting your arrival in awareness and acceptance. No matter what the apparent challenges and obstacles with which you may be faced along the way, know that "Spiritual Comfort" will provide means and methods for you to master them. In doing so, you will gradually, but inexorably, come into the mastership of the many dimensions of your self and eventually claim your inheritance as one who has moved from Self-Realization into God-Realization and beyond.

In your journeys know that Dan Rin is always with you. Look inside your heart and you will find him there.

~Sri Michael Owens

~*Editor's Note*~

The spiritual exercises, prayers, poems, and the conceptual index contained herein have been arranged by general topics of interest to spiritual seekers.

For your further contemplative study, the name of the Angel/Master of origin is listed at the end of each passage. Additional information on these and other Masters is contained in other books by Sri Michael.

Please note: For visual clarity, any discourse from the Angels/Masters is italicized; any words you are to speak are bolded and italicized.

~Table of Contents~

Chapter One

Connecting to the Light and Sound of God

Spiritual Comfort

Connecting with God's Will

♥ Connecting to the Heart of God with Universal Soul Movement

How Universal Soul Movement facilitates a connection with the Light and Sound leading all the way to the Heart of God

Love is the ultimate fuel that charges the Soul in its journeys to other realms and brings it closer to its selfless Godhood in the higher realms. The pure love of the transparent heart is the highest frequency exchange of the Light and Sound that can be experienced in the form of communication with the lower realms. As you lift your hearts to be touched by Sugmad, the Light and Sound sends through the opening of the heart a direct message from the center of beingness that It is present and is transmitting the highest frequency of Love to the Soul who is seeking the true, selfless connection to the Light and Sound. The Master can see and will grant passage to those who seek only to bring this great Love into existence in the hearts of all beings and be charged with the duty of transformation of the Light and Sound into accessible frequencies in the realms below the Great Divide to guide Souls that have not felt the complete warmth of Sugmad's presence in the universe. This Love is that which draws every being in existence back to the Heart of Sugmad.

~Master Rumi

♥ Connecting to the Heart of God with use of "HU"

The use of HU to return to God

HU is the sacred gift from the Sugmad to the great Souls of this universe that are ready to receive of the heart of Its truth. It is the final key to the highest plane in the long journey through all the lower realms of this universe and back to the heart of God in the Ocean of Love and Mercy. For those who deeply love Spirit and truth, then HU becomes the beacon by which their way is lit and guided and all other actions taken to follow where it leads. To truly love HU means to open all aspects of one's life and love and presence in every word that is spoken and every action that is taken in this plane and world or any other. HU is the key to man's return, and for those who truly love it and make it a part of themselves, they shall find ultimate success in their endeavors and trials along the path.

The Sugmad chose "HU" for one very simple reason. It is the cumulative and net sound of all other sounds, vibrations, and frequencies combined in one and refined to its pure essence as a master key to unlock the doors to each and every plane. Just as a locksmith creates specific keys for specific rooms, there are secret words and mantras to open specific planes and secret places in the universe. Like the master locksmith, he does create one key that is so subtle and perfect in design it will open any door to any room in which it is inserted. And so, "HU" is such a key and may be used to take the wielder to any place within the universe that he does have the merit and the ability to go.

Though the student may ask the question of why other words are needed in addition to HU, there are very good reasons why this must be the case. HU, though it can open every door as needed, does guide the student in a general way and can make specific journeys difficult or more complicated than need be. The secret words of the initiations do serve to identify your specific rank as Soul when you do travel to Inner realms. And though HU could be used to take you to the temple you do seek, without the proper identification of your merit and your rank, you yet may be refused the entrance you desire. As well, the secret words relate to specific energetic pathways and gates that are well known and traveled by others before. And this can make the success and ease of the intention much greater than otherwise it might be, if only the general power of HU were used to go and seek the destination of your heart. And so, as the student progresses on the path, one of the things he learns is when it is best to use the word of HU on general occasions or to manifest the Holy Spirit for protection from dark places, and when a specific word is used to follow a line of energy and safely and rapidly arrive at your goal and destination.

Also was this sacred word selected and chosen for its properties of aggregating light and transforming darkness, for like the alchemist's stone, it is the key to turning spiritual lead to gold and transmuting the dross of negativity and illusion into the heart of love and light. The HU is the water, the universal solvent of all negativity and pain and suffering. And so, for whatever trial is faced, whatever challenge rendered unto Soul, HU is given by Sugmad to light the way and open the heart to the path of higher understanding and love and the ability to take of proper action to guide the Soul back home.

When HU is sung, the Master frequency encoded in its many layers is transferred and becomes a part of the energetic bodies of man; and so, just as HU is the universal key to all life and the common denominator of existence in this universe, so does the student become connected to all life when this sacred word is sung and he becomes part of it and is, for a brief moment in time, connected to and enmeshed in the very fabric of existence and the heart of all life and all things. And so, HU is the key to connecting to the heart of the universe, and this always should be remembered when it is sung and the vistas of heaven are opened to the student.

~Sri Leytor

♥ Healing separation from God

A contemplative exercise that brings a direct connection with God's Will

Here is a contemplative exercise for any soul of any spiritual or religious affiliation who has been suffering from a sense of separation from God/Allah.

Part One:

1. Relax your entire body. You may say a prayer that has special meaning to you.

2. From your Heart of Hearts, commit your self, your every moment of this day and each day of your life hereafter to the Great One God, by any name that brings joy and recognition to your heart.

3. Breathe slowly, deeply, and rhythmically. On your in-breath and out-breath, slow and steady allow a soft and gently sound to emerge: *Aaaaaaaaaaahhhhhhhh laaaaahhhhh.* You may say or sing, *"With every breath I take, Allah, fill me with joy to do your will."*

4. Repeat for 5 to 20 minutes, depending upon your aptitude for such an exercise and increase your time in doing this each day to the desired amount. Play with it and make changes as guided.

We give to you a second part that may be added once the first has been practiced many times and begins to lose its potency.

Part Two:

Say or sing:

"On my out breath, I let go.

Enter joy, exit pain.

Enter love, exit fear.

Enter wisdom, exit ignorance.

Enter freedom, exit rigidity.

Enter light, exit darkness.

Enter music, exit deafness.

Fill me with your essence, Allah, and your attributes.

I devote myself as a flute for your song.

Play me, I humbly pray."

Of course, you must be willing to follow through with the promises inherent in this sequence. If you do, the flow of Divine Spirit will enter you and take over to the extent you allow it. Only then will you know that all that has been promised by Allah can be yours, as you become a beautiful and willing vehicle for It.

You may do this exercise with eyes closed in a deep meditative state, with eyes open in-between activities, or anytime you would like to tune into Allah. If you do begin with eyes closed and have some profound experiences, then please stay with it until it ceases to be effective. Keep it changing a bit. It is then you may use it in activity.

Of course, be careful to stay alert and in your body when operating a car or other heavy machinery. As you breathe in and out the essence of Allah, with the heartbeat of Allah as your own, you may begin to accept a much greater, vital, moment-to-moment, creative reality, a reality pregnant with possibility, joy, patience, and loving-kindness. Breathing in such a devoted and awakened state of awareness brings connection and humility. Humility purifies, clarifies, and respects the generosity of Allah. Humility enables one to remember Allah in every moment and thus glorify His presence.

This exercise is for you, the willing seeker, and is never to be forced upon another person. It is a gift that can only be accepted and cherished, as is your life.

~Archangel Gabriel

Connecting with the Heart Consciousness of Sugmad

Morning exercise with reactivation during day

Herein is a contemplative exercise that can place us in the highest aspect of the heart consciousness in our daily communications at work, with family and at play.

1. Each morning you must start with the acquisition of Sugmad's highest grace and place that within the center of your heart beingness.

2. After a ten-minute "**HU**" song, state out loud: "*I OPERATE THROUGH THE HEART CONSCIOUSNESS OF SUGMAD.*" <u>Do this three times.</u>

3. The reactivation mantra that you can use during your day is: "*TRESTE-TU-MASTE.*" Or you may simply repeat the affirmation in a quiet moment of your day.

~ Babaji

Spiritual Comfort

Connecting with the Word of God

- ♥ How contemplative prayer works
- ♥ Ignite the God power within

Contemplative prayer provides soul with the ability to know more of Allah, creation, and itself, and can be performed in any number of ways. Allah is the epitome of the imagination's ability to manifest and creativity. Likewise, as an individual soul and piece of Allah embodied in human form, each person can awaken and reignite this God-power within. How? Practice and become adept at this simple and fundamental gift: contemplative prayer. Contemplation is the mind and soul's ability to focus on and connect the participant with the Word of God.

1. Focus on the written, spoken, or intuitive word or Light and Sound as seen, heard, or sensed within.

2. Connect to the heart and unity of God.

3. Contemplate with eyes open more and more throughout the day and at least once per day for half an hour with eyes closed to awaken serenity, peace, and love within the heart. Daily worries keep the aspirant focused on externals and away from the core of the heart.

4. Take care of business, do the next right thing, and let it go.

5. Strive to remain alert in the midst of chaos and each waking moment. You can dialogue with Allah in any moment. To do so can bring great and everlasting joy, more real than what you have been experiencing. This will free the attention to return at any time to the bosom of Allah. With so many moments each day, there need be no idle time of boredom.

6. Contemplate the moment; seize the day!

7. Contemplate the words of the holy writings; contemplate what is happening inside your body, mind, and beingness. You may participate with the Word of God at any time. Just make it so. Simple.

~Archangel Gabriel

Contemplation – How To's

Explaining contemplation and the practicing steps of its use

We are all students of Sugmad's Love and contentment, and, even in the use of the tremendous love that is at hand, this study will demand a methodology of understanding its use and needs in daily life on all planes of existence.

Spiritual Comfort

The path to this understanding is availed by seeking within on the Inner Planes of awareness the guiding message that has been placed for your discovery.

1. Sit quietly with focus on your Third Eye and feel through your heart with eyes closed. This will open a new and wonderful communication with a part of your being that should just be coming into focus as a part of your awareness. From this place, the Light and Sound can begin to enter and add to your experiences in the Inner World and life that has been opening to you. To facilitate this experience, you may use the word **HU** as a mantra to bring greater intensity to your first efforts to contact the Inner Worlds of awareness.

2. You also may have been given a sacred word to use to help you to be in contact with the Living Sehaji Master on the Inner to bring you along this new path. Take what you find in this place and let your heart hear it and then write whatever may come to you about the experience. This is called contemplation. Unlike meditation, it allows for interaction with the energy that comes through the heart via the Light and Sound. This communication will give some answers and will offer some guidance from the Inner spiritual masters who step forward to aid in your journey toward the Heart of Sugmad. This is a place where the Living Sehaji Master, Dan Rin, will speak to

you and answer questions of the heart's expectations.

3. From this place, he will guide you to other Inner masters who will bring a new presence to the wisdom that is already within you on how to progress as you seek new levels of awareness in all realms of beingness.

4. Trust in what Dan Rin brings to you in these times of contemplation and use the guidance offered to you during this long and wonderful journey you have chosen to take in The Way of Truth.

The wisdom for your journey to your true self as Soul is of great benefit to all that may come into your path as you grow toward the God Worlds. Do not look to understand these things with the mind, for they are specifically tuned to be communicated through the heart. As you gain merit in your journeys, you will be given an understanding of your Soul mission in this Outer life in the Worlds of Illusion and Duality governed by Kal Niranjan, who oversees your karmic path as you progress on this road of awakenings. There are other levels of awareness that precede the steps into Soul consciousness which is placed from where even greater comprehension of the God power begins to enter into your being through the Light and Sound. The call to the higher realms of being will start to gain strength in you and the presence of Sugmad's Love will draw you closer to your true purpose of being in that love.

~Babaji

Contemplation and Universal Soul Movement

The relationship between contemplation and Universal Soul Movement

In contemplation comes the direction from the Living Master of the Light and Sound, Dan Rin, as to the purpose of your call to this way of life in The Way of Truth. The participants of this way of life have a very precise and well-defined mission - to bring the great love of Sugmad to all Souls that have been denied the warmth of Its immense power in their lives. The initiations that come are directed via the Inner awareness of the Living Master from the great ones that prepare you as Soul for your place in the higher realms of beingness. It is through contemplation that the necessary changes are made to karmic duties, the sensitivity to the new frequency of the Light and Sound and the ability to understand the knowledge that is being passed from entities of other origins than this universe, which sometimes are encountered during Universal Soul Movement.

The information needed to maintain the correct frequencies in the vortices that feed the healing energy to the Light and

Sound anchored in certain places in this universe and on this planet has to be maintained as part of the karmic duties of the participants of The Way of Truth. Dan Rin has gone through extensive training to be able to manipulate the Light and Sound and is the one who has brought it to the peak of efficiency in this temporal reality for the initiates to use in their duties here. During contemplation the student is trained by the Master to be of maximum use to this Sugmad.

~Dan Rin

Direct Connection with the Light and Sound of God

A step by step exercise with a mantra for the participant to use to make a direct connection with the Light and Sound

This exercise is intended to give the participant their first initiation when they use it. At this point if you have felt the touch of the Light and Sound and heard an Inner voice saying it is now your time, there is a simple step to take to begin to realize your true purpose in being and to start on a path that will revitalize your heart to the Love that has been yours through time immemorial.

This exercise is given by the Living Master of the Light and Sound, Dan Rin, as a way to open the door of your Sacred Heart so that it can be filled with the desire of contact with that which will move you into a state of wonderment and lead you to begin to walk the path before you in The Way of Truth.

1. Sit in contemplation using the Third Eye (the center of the temple between your eyebrows in the middle of your forehead) to focus on the heart within the center of your being.

2. Let your breathing be slow and steady.

3. The word "*HU*" has been mentioned before as a way to allow you to feel the love of Sugmad. Chant this word softly five times.

4. Then ask within your heart that the Living Master of the Light and Sound, Dan Rin, be present with you as you look into yourself to feel the love of Sugmad for the first time entering into your true being, that of Soul.

5. As you sit with your eyes closed, imagine a vibrant, gold light surrounding you. This is the presence of Dan Rin gently lifting you out of the illusion of the world of duality to show you for the first time in your heart the essence of your true self in Soul. Hold this feeling as long as you can.

6. After the contemplation, take pen and paper and, without thinking too much, write about your experience. Share this with no one. Repeat this

exercise for one week. You will feel your heart begin to open and may sense your first connection to the Light and Sound. This will be the beginning of your journey in The Way of Truth.

~Babaji

Enjoy Life

Here is a contemplative exercise that will enable the participant to connect with the joy of living

Let me give to you a way to maintain a spiritual awareness of joy in everyday life. Love those around you and give of the grace that Sugmad has placed in your heart. If you wish to infuse this into your consciousness, use this mantra as you awaken each morning before the thoughts of the day begin. After a "*HU*" song, say this once: "*NU-LETEN-NE*" (new-letten nā)

~Babaji

Expand Consciousness by Collapsing Time and Space

A contemplative technique for collapsing space and time:

1. Completely relax, devote yourself to Sugmad, and sing your secret word or "**HU.**"

2. Meet with a Master of your choice on your Inner screen.

3. Look at the clock with eyes open; then close them and continue. Imagine space and time being infinitely big, especially between moments. Feel the spaces between moments and enjoy the bliss of this. Make a postulate that you will feel wonderful exploring your Inner Worlds between moments and between spaces for the next 30 minutes of perceived time, but that it will only take 3 minutes of Earth time and that it will be very productive and exhilarating.

4. Expand out in consciousness into the farthest reaches of the known and unknown universes. Feel everything without fear. Grab hold of the edges of infinity and bring it back with you. Wrap eternity around you like a soft, warm robe, and wear it throughout the day.

5. Open your eyes and note the time. Carry the robe of eternity around you for the day, or at least the

next hour, in all you do. Every now and then, consider the time and how your perceptions match the moving of the clock.

6. Record your perceptions over the next few days. Experiment and find what works best for you.

~ Sri Leytor

Focus on Personal Mastership

♥ Virtues to focus on and develop

♥ Qualities of Sehaji Mastership

The virtues participants of The Way of Truth should be focusing on and what should be their perceived qualities of Sehaji Mastership

The participants of The Way of Truth should start by focusing on openhearted devotion and determined dedication to align with and do the will of the Father of All and the Sugmad in which they now live. They must seek to move beyond the boundaries of their own limitations, emotions, engrammatic stagnation, and skill development, to fight the forces of darkness within their own heart and Inner and Outer bodies. When the participant can conquer, with courage, the ravages done through time by their own failures and ignorance, only then shall they truly be able to embrace their own hearts and renew their sacred vows to the Greatest Heart of All. In this way, shall the participant be able to move into the higher realms where Mastery holds souls in its loving grasp. As Masters, we pledge our lives and efforts to doing the will of the Great One. For this, one must first conquer all fears and inability to accept mystery and lack of perfection. Now, please do not take what I am saying to mean that participants must be perfectly pure and masterfully capable of everything. This is, of course, not possible. In working moment to moment with the Inner masters, participants will come to know what they need to do, one step at a time. Taking each next step with an open heart and attitude of willingness will go a very long way toward making the changes that will be needed. Remember to live in the present moment with as much love and courage as you possibly can, dear participants. Cast your fears to the west wind and embrace the wind of change coming from the east, from the rising sun of new beginnings in each moment. What was once terrifying can become enjoyable. Each stepping stone combines to build a future foundation of greater structure for the temple of wisdom in you and in the Inner Worlds for all.

Additional qualities needed for Sehaji Mastership include agility, fortitude in the face of adversity, willingness to learn new fighting and protective skills, and use of these skills judiciously when absolutely necessary. When it gets out into the farthest reaches, Soul never knows when it might be attacked and need to use compassion, communication, negotiation, and invisibility. The flexibility and skills gained from each step of Souls' development on all levels of their lives can be coalesced and used in moving the universes forward, as is our plan. As you know, change very often encounters resistance and many souls with high status will feel threatened and retaliate with whatever methods they feel they need to use to keep changes that they dread from taking place. As Sehaji Masters, we understand that opposition is a way of life; we arm ourselves with a spectrum of skills to handle this resistance. We begin with the utmost love and gentleness, and only proceed to stronger methods if the opposing souls threaten our mission or us.

~Master Kusulu

Gaining a Glimpse of God-Realization

A contemplative technique that will give the participant a glimpse of God-Realization

1. Go into quiet contemplation and ask the Inner Master for a glimpse of God- Realization. Quietly within your own heart, envision a golden white light glowing, gaining in strength and momentum, flying out in all directions with the strength and force of a mother's love for her child.

2. Sing *"HU-ALAYHA"* for a few moments. You are a child of Sugmad.

3. Envision and feel the more powerful love of God, your parent, gently connecting to your heart, and

as you rejoin in full consciousness, thank the God who gives you continual life for the blessings bestowed upon you each day. Bless all inside you and all outside you, as you and God merge into an infinite golden globe of universal absorption.

~Dan Rin

Gaining Understanding in Art

A highly-detailed, step-by-step contemplative exercise that will develop a higher understanding of the aesthetics in the arts

To develop a higher understanding of the aesthetics in the arts, you may practice the following spiritual exercise:

1. Go within. Call upon me to meet you and feel a strong connection with me.

2. Sing your secret word or *"HU"* or this mantra: *"SANG-HU-AH-HA"* several times.

3. Imagine yourself peaceful, fully present, and in unity with the finished product, whether it is an artistic expression of another or your own finished or desired creation. You may contemplate on the drawing of me with the Star Tetrahedron in

addition to the finished product, or the Star Tetrahedron alone, if you like.

4. Feel a rhythm, pulse, meter, and cadence — 1 2 3, 1 2 3, 1 2 3, flowing along a river of God's love. Down from the highest, down to the physical and up again. 1, 2, 3 — the same and ever-changing, and pulsing with joy – move with it!

5. Expand. Use all your senses with each work. In contemplation, dance with a painting with color and form. Listen to colors and hear what they have to say. See the colors of a musical piece. Feel the molecules within the piece resonate and dance with molecules, atoms, and quarks within you. You change the piece and your own consciousness with this highly conscious interaction.

6. Go into it all the way and ride on the stream of the Holy Spirit back through all the planes, straight into the heart of Sugmad.

7. Use the art piece as a springboard of Sugmad's creation to know Itself. You, as creator or observer, become a spiritual participant in this movement of joy for yourself and as a trailblazer for others. Once you have gone where no soul has gone before, others may follow. Move and rest and be at peace in the neutrality of this esoteric experience.

8. Look also to nature to affirm and expand your artistic expressions. Make love to the piece, with your consciousness carefully caressing every aspect, and allow it to unfold in rapture.

~ Master Agnotti

The Purpose of Love

What the participants of The Way of Truth can do to bring themselves into higher spiritual ground

First, you must decide what you are here for. Do you love God? Then devote every thought, word, and deed in every moment of your day to doing the will of the First Cause, the Great One, Sugmad, with the highest love for all of life, for the highest good of all concerned. Do the spiritual exercises outlined in The Way of Truth materials and manuals. Practice daily. These exercises are starting points; be creative and go with your experiences. Develop your own. This is essential and cannot be emphasized enough. You must stay open in your heart and mind in order to let soul lead the way and be connected to the rest of the spiritual hierarchy. We are not trying to develop an army of clones. You are unique as Soul. You are being called to action. We need you and your unique talents and skills, your own brand of love and service. Do what works for you.

Do what you love, what you are already developed to do. You do not need to look or act like anyone else. You must develop "you" to the highest degree possible. This is crucial. If you don't already, then love yourself! You are not here to take orders from anyone but your own higher self and Sugmad. You decide. If you are still experiencing lots of problems with your life, then reach out to others who have passed that way before and who can empathize and lend you their experience, strength and hope. Heal yourself so you can move onto your altruistic dreams. You are here to be part of a larger whole. As soon as you can, do what you can. You do not have to be wholly healed to start. Just start, this moment. Your healing will increase a thousand fold with your generous giving and helping others. Move into your Highest Self. Celebrate yourself as Soul, a beloved child of God. Celebrate your brothers and sisters, especially those you love to hate. They are Soul, too. Leave them alone if they are threatening or harmful, but send them compassionate goodwill and let it go. It might sound like a worn out cliché, but it is true - it is all about love!

~Master Towart Managi

Moving through the Dark Night of Soul

♥ Releasing pain and stagnation

The antidote for darkness is light, awareness, and freedom. Remember that the Light, Music, and Love of Allah are ever available to all, ever broadcasting, as waves of energy from the sun. As night on Earth, darkness is a temporary illusion, a passage in the cycle of time, created by being in the shadow of something blocking out the light and warmth that is freely available when the blocking object is removed.

1. Contemplate on what it is within your own self that blocks Allah from penetrating every part of your being. No one can keep you from Allah but yourself.

2. Allow yourself to know yourself.

3. Decide what you want.

4. Recognize that the worlds upon worlds were not built to your specifications, but to the Great One who created all. You are part of the All, not the other way around. If you open yourself, discipline yourself, do your daily spiritual practice with fervor and joy, you may see the Inner sun rise, the gates of heaven open, and Allah rushing in.

5. If you do all the spiritual practices you know and still do not get the result you seek, then know that what is supposed to be for you at this time is already here, and all is well and as it should be. Allah's wisdom is far beyond your own and all is in the perfection of Allah in the grand scheme of things.

6. Do not let preconceptions or other people's experiences set a standard for you. The worlds are

vast and you are unique. Your history determines what happens to you today. What you do today extends your history or changes it. It is up to you.

7. Do not let appearances fool you. Hold fast to a devoted spiritual practice. Hold fast to Allah and His Love and Mercy. His gifts do not come exactly as we think they should many times, but when they come, the gifts do exceed all expectation in reward. Trust.

8. You may do whatever daily devotional you choose.

9. Here is a powerful mantra to chant or sing: *"LA-BAY-KA-ALLAH, UMA-LA-BAY-KA."* It means, "Here I am, Allah, in thy presence." Here I am, here you are; we are together. We are One. Sing it as you celebrate your life! Live with joy! Allow Allah to enter your heart. Surrender all else to Allah every morning upon arising, with the rising of the sun, and every evening upon retiring to bed, and in as many moments throughout the day that you remember to do so.

10. Forget right or wrong in this practice; let go of rigidity. Let go of preconceptions. Do it with sincerity and humility for the good of all creation. And remember – darkness and light go hand in hand in the Earth plane. Every person alive

contends with both. When one stands straight and tall, with unwavering faith and love, in the center and balance of opposites, one will open to amazing joy and blessings.

11. May you enjoy the joy that is available to you today! Blessed Be.

~Archangel Gabriel

♥ Removing Hurt and Debris from Past Hurt

1. Gently close your eyes.

2. Sing "*HU*" three times.

3. Focus in on what may ail you, no matter how little, how large or how small. Focus on something you want to go away.

4. Say this postulate inwardly (take the mind picture you have within) and say "*GO AWAY, YOU DO NOT EXIST.*"

5. Verbally say: "*My sky is open and clear. My heart is free, so leave in the name of the most holy. I do not recognize you.*"

6. Sing "*HU*" three times.

7. Now imagine the clouds of pain and disappointment disappearing from your sky. See a blue clear sky, it is that simple.

Blessed Be.

~St. Jerome

Removing Obstacles from the God Seeker's Environment

To see the root of an obstacle and remove it from your physical through your spiritual environments, there are three simple, but not necessarily easy, steps to follow: Be, feel, and do.

1. You must first be full of the purest Light and Sound from your Sugmad's Great Heart. Many teachers have taught you how to reach into the very heart and soul of the Divine Ocean of Unconditional Love and Mercy. Go there now and fill up as you would a tank of gas in your car.

2. Call upon Dan Rin, another Sehaji Master, and/or myself, and feel the presence of that soul next to or within your heart. If you invite us into your very body, we will come with all respect and train soul for greater illustration of how to do these things. You might choose to feel us within every cell of your beingness for greater effect.

3. See and feel a new spectrum of pure Light and Sound, which is calibrated higher and finer than you have ever seen before, vibrating within your heart. The Light is not blinding but is very strong.

4. Sing: *"AH-LAYA-HU."* Very important: The syllables **"AH LAYA"** are to be sung or heard on the in-breath; "HU" is not sung with the vocal chords, but by blowing the breath out of the mouth. (Some sounds that work best are not easily described by Earth languages, so experiment with the sounds.)

5. Hold this state of consciousness and the unusual image of this calibration in your Third Eye, your heart, and your solar plexus for as long as you can. Put this level of purest Divine Light and Sound in every corner of your beingness - past, present, and future.

6. You may see the root lifting and letting go of its long hold and dissolving into the nothingness from which it came. You may hold a sword or sharp bladed gyro to cut through tenacious roots and chords with the Master's permission. DO NOT RETRIEVE your obstacle or talk about it again, or you can take it back again.

7. Take as long as you need for this exercise. You may do it with eyes open or eyes closed. Come back to it weekly for as long as you need to remove any dross that clings and prevents your return as a Warrior for the Holiest One. After you have removed as many of your obstacles as

you can perceive, come see me, if you choose to do so, and we can commence further training. Welcome to our worlds, young Sehaji Master.

~Sri Kusulu

A Prayer for Peace, Love, and Greater Brotherhood for Humanity

Heavenly Father, when I seek peace
*Let me **give peace** to those in strife;*
When I seek love, let me give love
To a motherless child.

*When I seek forgiveness, let me **forgive** the one*
Who has transgressed against me and left
me brokenhearted.
And when I want comfort, let me find the soul
Whose heart is emptier than mine and give them solace.

Father, make me an instrument of Thy peace,
*As Brother Francis has prayed; and let me **be the One***
*Who opens the door and shines the light of hope and **giving***

Spiritual Comfort

For the weary traveler who seeks rest in
the impending night.

Lead me to understand the stone in my brother's heart;
And let me not fall upon it, but lift it out
*And cast it away into the Ocean of Love and **Thy Mercy**,*
So that he can feel the lightness of your loving grace.

Father, let there be a star in heaven
For every soul on earth;
*And let each star **be the guiding light** for that soul*
To find their way back to your loving arms.

Let every person I encounter
Feel the weight of their burdens slip away
By the simple act of a kind word or smile
*Given from my Heart, which is **from Your Heart**,*
in your Blessed Name.

Chapter Two

Communing with the Sehaji Masters

Spiritual Comfort

Commune with the Grand Council

Here follows a contemplative technique that expands the participant into a feeling of Oneness with the Grand Council Heart Consciousness:

1. Imagine yourself lying on a grassy knoll on a warm, sunny day. You are gazing at the peaceful blue sky and from the far horizon there comes an eagle flying into your range of vision. Watch it fly overhead as it casts a golden aura over the lands with its tremendous and powerful wings.

2. Merge your consciousness with this graceful creature that represents the spiritual heart of the Grand Council. Simply watch it fly and feel yourself soaring with it above the clouds. At the same time, say this mantra aloud three times: *"SIVA-TU-ONA-HU-LE."*

3. Watch the eagle and become one with its majestic journey across the horizon. Ask for a member of the Grand Council to speak to your heart about what you most need to know in this moment of time.

4. Stay in contemplation until the eagle leaves the sky and you have a message imprinted upon your heart. Blessed Be.

~Master Milarepa

Communicate with the Masters

The White Robe Tradition

If you would like to visit with the Masters of Sat Nam's Court, this is an exercise that will open your consciousness to what they want to share with you.

These are the steps to the contemplative exercise:

1. Sing the name of Spiritual Master Dan Rin five times.

2. Sing "*HU*" five times.

3. Allow your attention to drift to the Inner screen of the mind. Begin to visualize what the Court would look like to you. Ask to be shown any information necessary for your spiritual growth. Be prepared to meet with a member of the Court and be escorted onto its grounds. Stay in contemplation for at least twenty minutes. Do not be disappointed if your visual or auditory experience is less than vivid.

4. Know that you are having the experience because the Sehaji Masters are committed to your growth and to your becoming a member of their ranks.

~Dan Rin

Spiritual Comfort

Contemplative Exercise with Master Towart Managi

A contemplative exercise to uplift the heart, develop more hope and love, and give the God seeker more enriching alternatives regarding their spiritual and material survival

Dear Ones, we are the conduits of God's Great Love. You may say these lines as an opening prayer - "*I devote my every breath, heartbeat, and life's song to the Great One God. I open and live in this One Love, here and now. Let all fears and concerns vanish like shadows in the Fullness of Light and Love. The Holy Spirit guides and protects me.*"

1. Relax completely. Imagine standing with Dan Rin and me at a point high above the Earth, over your homeland, looking down upon her from afar. See, feel, and hear the Light and Sound of Sugmad filling our hearts and beating with the rhythm of our hearts and the spheres of the heavens above and within.

2. See the Light and Sound of Sugmad in various luminous colors surrounding the entire Earth, enfolding the Earth in radiant yet gentle hues and tones, pulsing with life and love and encouragement. Sing "*AH-SWAY-LO,*" 3 times. Feel oneness in connection with the healing flow of Sugmad's Great Love into the Earth plane.

Know that you are a true warrior of the heart and conduit for Sugmad's love.

3. Continue to feel and participate in the energetic exchange between the triad of the three of us and the triad of Sugmad, Earth, and us. We are three within three. All that is not love cannot stand the heat and energetic pulse of love, and will wither and die and be dissolved into the great stream of God's love pouring through your heart. Know that the entire spiritual hierarchy loves you and wants to help you succeed, if your heart is pure and in alignment with the love and enrichment of all life. Enjoy this exercise and practice it often throughout your day.

Blessed Be, Dear Ones. I send the greatest love from the Father of All to you, always.

~Master Towart Managi

Experience the God Worlds

A step-by-step contemplative exercise that will give the seeker an experience in the God Worlds

This is an ancient mantra to open the heart to the vibratory understanding of the language of the Masters and all those who speak from the Inner spiritual realms as to what direction we're moving in, and to offer us guidance:

"MISRADU-MISRADU-MISRADU-KU." This allows the dialect of the Ancient Ones to be understood in the purest vibratory forms, but allows a useable translation for the mind to implement the methods given to accelerate your movement into the God Worlds. This is offered to those with the attitude of the pure, open, selfless transparent heart that seeks only to return home to the love of Sugmad.

1. Use *"HU"* to center your consciousness in the sacred heart and to open the channel to the way of the Masters.

2. Use this mantra <u>three times</u> *"MISRADU - MISRADU - MISRADU - KU"* and sit in quiet contemplation to understand that which is beyond knowing: *"Su lot tilnot tu dess tra dos tu dente neste' alt tente daspensé ot notē tel-lettis ma-ettas nus delmsi te."* This is a sample that was transmitted and left in its original dialect. (This spelling is the best that can be given.) It is a simple greeting to you who have chosen to walk in the higher realms of God Awareness.

3. Repeat it the best you can and feel the change in your heart vibration.

~Babaji

Experience Soul Movement

A contemplative exercise to open the door to a greater conscious state of Soul Movement

1. Sit comfortably and take several deep breaths until you feel relaxed. Sing *"HU"* five times.

2. Imagine you are standing on a bluff over a calm, blue sea with soft white clouds that are tinged with the colors of dawn. It is early morning.

3. Take into your lungs the freshness of the new day and look across the great expanse of moving, living waters. These are the waters of soul. There are no boundaries, no land anywhere. It is all the living, breathing sea of your consciousness. Enjoy the sense of freedom for a few minutes. Now prepare to dive into that sea.

4. Say the mantra: *"SU-LI-PRANA-O-TE"* (pronounced "soo lee prahnah oh tay") three times very slowly.

5. Now dive from the bluff into the great expanse of your consciousness and immerse yourself in the waves of awareness that catch you and lift you and hold you like a floating ball of light. Simply allow yourself to float and move with the waves of your beingness.

6. Feel that you are expanding into this ocean of oneness with your true self. Everything seems sharper and; sounds are more musical, colors are more brilliant. The sun's warmth on your body soothes your senses as gentle breezes open your consciousness to more feeling and receptivity.

7. Stay in this heightened state of awareness for the next 20 minutes. Allow whatever comes through to play on the screen of your Third Eye. You may also ask a question about anything in your life.

8. Then continue to float peacefully on the gentle waters and listen to the Inner depths of your heart as it speaks to you. Blessed be.

~Dan Rin

Find your Spiritual Mission and Purpose

A step by step contemplative exercise that will assist participants in finding their spiritual mission and purpose

1. Stand on a beautiful mountaintop surveying all the countryside and your life from beginning to end.

2. Feel the embrace of Sri Dan Rin and myself. We three make a powerful trinity, in which you may move in the direction of your heart.

3. Let us dance - we three together, with you in the middle - with all hearts wide open, connected, and flowing with Sugmad's great love.

4. Let us sing "*BEL-LA-HU*" together in joy and recognition and celebration!

5. Allow your purpose to come into your Inner sight and fill your heart with gladness. Allow quietude for 20 - 30 minutes until Spirit sees otherwise.

6. Be sure to write down your experiences - do not allow the joy and realness of this experience to slip away.

7. Welcome to your true spiritual mission and cause. Welcome to the kindred spirits of the Sehaji!

~Master Arutu

Glimpse the Face of God

Here follows a contemplative exercise with a mantra that will give the God seeker a glimpse of God Consciousness

1. Imagine sitting in a darkened movie theater. The massive curtains slowly pull away from the screen and there is a bright, white field on which an image will soon come into view.

2. Concentrate on the white screen before you and say this mantra three times: *"SU-LE-TA-VIYU-NAM-SUGMAD"* (pronounced "soo lay tah veeyoo nahm soogmahd.")

3. Simply continue to watch this Inner screen of light until the Face of God begins to appear. It may look like a simple blue spot or circle; or it may look like stars or colored lights; or you may see two brilliant eyes gazing into your heart. Whatever form it takes, The Face of God will always remain a puzzle yet to be completed and does not appear the same way to any two souls, but It will reveal a part of Itself to the true God seeker who is ready for a glimpse of God Consciousness.

~Dan Rin

Reach God-Realization with the Number 9

The secret behind "9" and how can we use it to reach God-Realization

The Nine Silent Ones have mastered the Law of Silence, the Law of Three, and the Law of Cause and Effect, principally, among other fundamental spiritual laws. They have much to teach you, the aspirant, should you wish to contact them in their periods of silence. However, do not attempt to do so unless you are very serious and committed to the training you will get. As Paulji (Paul Twitchell) pointed out in his discourse on 9, there is a rhythm to the initiations in the pattern of three. Each set of three teaches certain principles and lays the foundation for the next set; the first two culminate in the third; the fourth and fifth culminate in the sixth, and so on. We must each contemplate with the Living Sehaji Master as to what our initiations mean to us individually and collectively as souls awakening, and also what our initiations mean to Sugmad.

There is a profound fluidity to be found within the rhythm of three: positive, negative, neutral - inflow, outflow, stillness - you, me, God. Focus on any pair of opposites and their union. From two comes an independent third; that's the foundation of creation. From union of man and woman comes an independent child. Three dimensions create the physical plane. Instructors teach basic dance steps from repetition of 1, 2, 3. Some say there is a very good reason that animals and humans are designed with two ears and one mouth; it is twice as important to listen as to speak.

Spiritual Comfort

Try it for yourself for two hours per day, at the hour of nine, for at least three weeks and see what changes come about in you. Practice this: write and learn more from your rhythmic typing or pen motions, tapping on a hard surface, or dancing or stepping in uniform beat as you walk or skate or row or swim. Words cannot convey direct experience, dear souls, but you can and will discover a new world of understanding with focus on "3 in 3" and 9 in the intimate workings of your daily life. Not only will all your problems fade without your constant focus, but the worlds of Sugmad will open as you align your body with it. Partly you will notice a soothing flow that you can get into, which stills the gnawing of the emotions and mind; partly a calming order takes over that you can rely on as no other; partly you will burst through barriers not previously transparent to you as you take your next step. These disciplines convey silent appreciation and gratitude, elevating rhythm, learning your own heartbeat, and marrying your beat with the grand beat in others and in God. Good stuff!

~Master Pythagoras

Chapter Three

Health and Spiritual Balance

~Cleansing~

Beginning Your Day – Cleansing Mental Body

For daily practice to rid the self of ego and Maya and illusion, the following technique may be practiced.

1. First, each day at rising, or when beginning preparations for work, or to begin each daily undertaking, take a quiet moment alone and gently sing *"HU"* or the sacred word of your initiation to polarize your subtle bodies with the radiance and love of God.

2. And then, after a few moments, declare within yourself that you seek to see and experience only truth within this day.

3. And with practice and diligence the lower bodies shall begin to be trained to repel the negative forces and keep The Way of Truth well lit.

~Sri Leytor

Dealing with Difficulties – Mental, Emotional, & Physical Bodies

♥ Keep the heart free from distractions

♥ See the truth within illusion

A technique for daily practice that may be used when you do encounter some difficulty or obstacle upon your path of daily living is the following:

1. Quietly to yourself sing five of the sacred "**HU**s."

2. Then in your imagination, ask the Master to come to you and sweep away any illusion and show you only truth, that your heart should not become obstructed, and you might only know the peace and joy and ecstasy that comes from an open heart and a connection to Sugmad's love.

~Sri Leytor

Spiritual Comfort

Purifying - Mental, Emotional, & Physical Bodies

- ♥ Resolve personal problems
- ♥ Develop personal coping skills in daily life

1. Sing **"AH-LA-HEEM."**

2. Ask Allah for help and imagine going to a rejuvenating spa of great beauty on the Inner Planes.

3. Imagine Allah washing you clean, as you stand in a fountain of pure light and sound.

4. Imagine Allah changing you, as a master surgeon, gently, almost imperceptibly but powerfully and permanently, manipulating your energetic signature in order for you to resolve personal problems.

5. Do this contemplative exercise once per day for as long as you can stay with it, with eyes closed for a week. Imagine that you are becoming the greatest you that you have ever been, that your problems are being lifted out, as you are ready to let them go.

6. Then throughout the day, act with love shining from your heart and eyes. Move in new and creative ways.

7. Allow Allah to use you as you perform your daily tasks with a new level of love and creativity. You are a new person on the inside and it will show! You can sing or dance, draw or write poetry to express this newfound way of being.

8. Take action to balance the new energies in you to reinforce the new ways of being into your physical body and mind.

9. Be patient, believers and lovers of truth! With Allah, all things are possible! If you wish to resolve problems, you can do it -- in alignment with Allah.

~Archangel Gabriel

Unrestricting the Flow of God Energy - Physical Body

♥ Open root chakra

♥ Ground God energy to Physical Plane

Contemplation 1:

Always there are opportunities to make progress towards the goal. Clearing the root chakra is merely one stop on the path back to God. There are many others. At times, there will be the need for this exercise. Many have great difficulty allowing the God-energy to pass freely through them. This wisdom is thus very important to man.

1. Begin by imagining yourself to be a column of light.

2. Then move slowly down until you reach the lowest level, the root chakra.

3. Begin to see a gently pulsing wave of energy slowly moving up the column of light and back down again. This up-and-down rhythmical wave motion gently dislodges and dissolves blockages and opens the chakras to greater flows of Light and Sound.

4. End by withdrawing the column upward, slowly leaving a clear open expression of space at each level.

5. Repeat this exercise several times over the course of a few weeks.

~Master Agnotti

Contemplation 2:

1. To clear this chakra, do as has been instructed in the above exercise.

2. It also helps, though, to chant or repeat the secret word or *"HU"* as the exercise is undertaken. This brings added strength to the process and more efficiently removes blockages and dross.

3. Do this several times over the course of a few weeks or until a lightness is felt.

~Master Agnotti

~Developing Spiritual Stamina~

Contemplations

Why contemplative exercises are recommended daily

This Inner world that has just been opened to you is vast and wonderful, but must be traveled with the help of the Living Sehaji Master, Dan Rin, for in your journey here you will encounter things that will be of great force and new to your consciousness.

The daily practice of contemplation is like any other process of learning, and, if practiced well, it will result in great benefits. As Dan Rin shows to you the methods to reach the place of knowledge necessary for your unfoldment, he will leave you with instructions on how to return to these Temples of Wisdom and archives of knowledge.

Through the daily practice of contemplation, you shall receive much of the training that is being offered to you on this path to God-Realization. As you are new to this process of awakening, it is necessary to re-visit these temples to gain from the knowledge that can be placed in your consciousness there. If you wish to be filled with the wonders of the Inner realms, the practice of daily contemplation will strengthen your ability to bring more of your experience to the lower levels of consciousness from which you operate in your daily life.

The wisdom for your journey to your true self as Soul is of great benefit to all that may come into your path as you grow toward the God Worlds. Do not look to understand these things with the mind, for they are specifically tuned to be communicated through the heart. As you gain merit in your journeys, you will be given an understanding of your Soul mission in this Outer life in the Worlds of Illusion and Duality governed by Kal Niranjan, who oversees your karmic path as you progress on this road of awakenings. There are other levels of awareness that precede the steps into Soul consciousness which is placed from where even greater comprehension of the God power begins to enter into your being through the Light and Sound. The call to the higher realms of being will start to gain strength in you and the presence of Sugmad's Love will draw you closer to your true purpose of being in that love.

~Master Kusulu

Mantras/Prayers

Use a mantra during contemplations and throughout your day

Any rhythmic and harmonic pulse that can cause in the heart a desire to be closer to the Light and Sound can be called a mantra.

The use of such a word or sound is the doorway in your contemplation that allows Soul to be released from the present situation that the lower bodies may be engaged in so that it may move unencumbered through the higher realms of being.

1. In your morning contemplation, you seek to understand what is to be a part of your mission each day to spread the Love of Sugmad and to bring it forward in your consciousness to be used during the course of the day.

2. The use of *"HU"* or your Sacred Word spoken inwardly will bring the vibration to the encounter that you have been led to as part of your daily, karmic duty as a carrier of the Light and Sound in The Way of Truth and releases the Love of Sugmad into the exchange taking place.

This effect is carried to all realms and brings greater stability to the infusion of the Light and Sound in this

Spiritual Comfort

universe and to this planet as this great healing of the karmic past takes place through the city of Ekere Tere.

~Master Rebazar Tarz

Morning Prayer

♥ Remember hope and your purpose here

♥ Maintain your heart as a spiritual warrior

We are the lights of Sugmad's love. We must be the beacons that will guide those still in the darkness and those still in slumber. Those Souls in spiritual recline need the lights to point the way to break the karmic cycles of those whose hearts are ready to make the journey. We carry Sugmad's sword with the recalibrated energies of the new path of the Light and Sound to relieve the unnecessary suffering and imbalances of this world.

1. Every morning say this postulate:

"The Sugmad is my sword
The Living Master is my Shield
The Holy Spirit is my Armor
And the Sehaji is my guidance into the
Light and Sound of God."

2. Afterwards sing *"HU"* five times and meet the challenges of your day!

~Dan Rin

Prayer for Retiring (and Awakening)

♥ How to encourage peace between Jews and Moslems

♥ How to heal your own heart

I give this prayer to all peoples of Earth to be sung upon awakening and before retiring each night, to encourage peace and brotherhood between Jews and Moslems. Healing begins within one's own heart.

Please feel free to change the name "Allah" to any that feels most comfortable. Allah cares not what you call Him, only that you heed His call.

Love's Inspiration to the Children of Abraham

"Dearest Beneficent and Merciful Allah,

I declare myself to be your glove

For Your wisdom, truth, and love.

Fill my whole body full of Light

For all are equal in your sight!

Spiritual Comfort

May peace be born of Moslem and Jew.

May all awaken to honor You.

When we embrace the brotherhood of man,

We'll meet in the heart of the Great I AM.

Please remind me when my heart turns cold,

That my brother's hands were made to hold.

Though children of an earthly mother,

All derive from One Holy Father.

No matter what the time of day

Help me always choose to say:

I give and receive love to each their fill.

I choose this moment to obey Your will."

~Archangel Gabriel

Protection – Mental Body

How to protect the mind's energy field from other's influences

A contemplative technique that protects the God seeker from the throes of practitioners of the right and left hand paths

Those that seek to disrupt the focus of the God seeker's resolve usually bring a disturbance into the energy field of the mind. Found here is a Buddhist mantra for peace, which is the best defense against a disturbance: **"OHM-SHAANTI-SHAANTI."**

~Babaji

~Expressing Sugmad through the Arts~

Find the pure love of Sugmad in expression

[From a retreat, Sri Michael speaking:]

1. Gently close your eyes.

2. Sing "*HU*" three times.

3. As I say these words, say [them] inwardly and see a light, a light, pouring into your heart, and it

comes directly from the Ocean of Love and Mercy, from our Beloved God, also known as Sugmad. Repeat after me inwardly: *"I am the beginning; I am an essence of eternity; through me is offered that which is absolute truth; in my arts is an expression of Spirit's works, and in it is found the purest love of Sugmad."*

4. Outwardly repeat after me: *"I see, I feel, and I am this Love. I see, I feel, and I am this Love. I see, I feel, and I am this Love."*

5. Sing *"HU"* three times.

Blessed be.

~Dan Rin

Chapter Four

Soul Consciousness and Self-Realization

Spiritual Comfort

Access Inner Wisdom

A spiritual exercise on how to access your Inner keys of wisdom

1. Imagine five golden keys in your Inner vision, each one sitting in the lock of a separate door. You have only to turn the key to open that particular door. Each door represents one of the spiritual virtues of wisdom: Love, Service, Surrender, Faith, and Honor.

2. Go to the first door of Love and say this mantra: *"AH-SE-TU-BA-FLO-RE-SET,"* then turn the key, open the door, and step across the threshold. What is the first thing you see as you step through the doorway? What is waiting on the other side? Write down whatever images or feelings come to you.

3. Then do the same thing with the other four keys and use the same mantra each time. This will bring into your daily awareness the flow and creativity of the spiritual keys of wisdom that are already part of your higher consciousness. Blessed be.

~Dan Rin

Soul Consciousness and Self-Realization

Associate Your Self with Africa's Renaissance

What it means to be associated with and an integral part of Africa's Renaissance

To be associated with and an integral part of Africa's Renaissance means to heal all manner of illness in body, mind and emotion, and to let go of the waste of the past. It means to grow into your fullness and wholeness as a human being, with soul "up front and center" leading the way. It means knowing who you are, what you came here to do, what you are willing to do, and what you are capable of doing. It means to commit to helping your fellow human beings, no matter the color of their skin, the style of their clothes, sound of their music, lifestyle, culture or mindset. It means loving all life and lending a helping hand in whatever way you can. It does not mean you must be perfect or a saint. If we waited until then, the army would be few indeed. Humans must help humans; soul helps soul.

What are you doing with your life? How much time do you waste on fruitless actions or emotions, obsessing, worrying, self-indulgence or any other manner of spinning your wheels? Lay down your destructive tools of the past – your addictions, your ignorance, your weapons of small or mass destruction, your greed, your anger, your attachment to your hedonistic fantasies. If Africa is the heart, soul, and mother of humanity then how are you willing to help your mother? To be an integral part you must be ready, willing and committed to waking up to who you truly are. You must be willing to accept your brothers and sisters as unique and different from yourself, equal and deserving of all good things, like you are. If you live in abundance in a thriving nation and have the creature comforts and financial means, then what are you willing to do to lend a hand to your brethren across the seas? If you live in abundance in Africa, what will you do to help alleviate some suffering next door to you?

This means - COME ALIVE FULLY AND COMPLETELY. Wake up! Come out and play! Find your place and take a stand! Move forward! Come out and dance with us! Roll up your sleeves and help the medical community. Activists, we need you. Look to your heart and work with the spiritual hierarchy, the political community, the non-governmental agencies, the schools, and the people. Be creative. Find your way.

~Master Towart Managi

Herein follows a contemplative exercise that will enable those who have the purity of heart the means to work with Arutu and Towart Managi in this spiritual movement for Africa's Renaissance

1. Imagine you are on a small boat or canoe which is gliding silently along a peaceful river. There is a definite destination ahead and you can feel it pulling you along effortlessly; it fills you with

increasing peace and joy the closer you get to it. The sounds of the waters are like a lullaby to the soul and you are serenely guided and protected on this journey. You have only to surrender, relax, and go with the flow of the river.

2. Now you come to a bridge that crosses over the river. Two Masters stand at the center of the bridge - Arutu and Towart Managi. They smile and raise their hands in greeting. As they do, your boat is guided to the riverbank and you get out and walk to the bridge. As you step onto it, say this mantra three times: *"SULU-TU-MANA-TU-ARA-TE."*

3. Now you are free to approach the Masters and they embrace you warmly. **Ask what you can do to help them in the spiritual movement toward the great African Renaissance.** That is all that is required, dear Brothers and Sisters of the Light and Sound. May God bless you in all that you do in His Holy Name.

~Dan Rin

Spiritual Comfort

Attain Self-Realization

The intent of this prayer song focuses on the attainment of Self-Realization

1. Sing *"HU"* five times and contemplate this prayer, line by line or as a whole.

> *In stillness, I know within my heart*
>
> *That I am needed within God's Will.*
>
> *Sensing within my most cherished part,*
>
> *I move in deeper still.*
>
> *Catching waves of love that are flowing,*
>
> *Coursing, moving in, around, and through,*
>
> *My senses reel; I feel it glowing*
>
> *Frequencies made of HU*
>
> *For I am soul, and now know this well.*
>
> *Being still, I let go of my past.*
>
> *I feel such love move within and swell,*
>
> *As my heart blooms at last.*
>
> *Trusting my impressions, this is how*
>
> *I sing HU and show my place in God.*

2. Conclude the prayer with five more long and loving rounds of **HU**.

~Dan Rin

Bring Africa's Renaissance Forward into Higher Ground

What the participants of The Way of Truth can do to bring this Renaissance forward into higher spiritual ground

First, you must decide what you are here for. Do you love God? Then devote every thought, word and deed in every moment of your day to doing the will of the First Cause, the Great One, Sugmad, with the highest love for all of life, for the highest good of all concerned. Do the spiritual exercises outlined in The Way of Truth materials and manuals. Practice daily. These exercises are starting points; be creative and go with your experiences. Develop your own. This is essential and cannot be emphasized enough. You must stay open in your heart and mind in order to let soul lead the way and be connected to the rest of the spiritual hierarchy. We are not trying to develop an army of clones. You are unique as soul. You are being called to action. We need you and your unique talents and skills, your own brand of love and service. Do what works for you.

Do what you love, what you are already developed to do. You do not need to look or act like anyone else. You must develop "you" to the highest degree possible. This is crucial. If you don't already, then love yourself! You are not here to take orders from anyone but your own higher self and Sugmad. You decide. If you are still experiencing lots of problems with your life, then reach out to others who have passed that way before and who can empathize and lend you their experience, strength, and hope. Heal yourself so you can move onto your altruistic dreams. You are here to be part of a larger whole. As soon as you can, do what you can. You do not have to be wholly healed to start. Just start, this moment. Your healing will increase a thousand fold with your generous giving and helping others. Move into your Highest Self. Celebrate yourself as soul, a beloved child of God. Celebrate your brothers and sisters, especially those you love to hate. They are soul, too. Leave them alone if they are threatening or harmful, but send them compassionate goodwill and let it go. It might sound like a worn out cliché, but it is true - it is all about love!

~Master Towart Managi

Communicate with Your Self as Soul

A contemplative exercise to develop a greater communication with soul

1. Visualize a cross section of a nautilus shell. The internal spiral spins on a central axis, which extends straight into your heart.

2. Watch the shell rotate, and draw the structure closer to your body.

3. Feel the rotation and your new ability to move inside it, from one portion or section to another, in and out of center, safe within and free to move.

4. This is your life, your Inner and Outer life and lower bodies. You can stay central and move the shell near or far; you can step inside and slow or increase the spin. You are in control.

5. You are soul and can experience any and all parts of this exercise as you wish. You cannot be harmed, and need not react as you would physically. You can view this experience from any angle you wish. No matter what happens, you chose where you are and what your response will be. You choose. You decide. You align with the rotation or not. You are soul, an integral part of the Great One.

6. You may sing the following mantra aloud or silently: *"TU-TE-AH-SA-ALL-LA-DEMOS."*

~Dan Rin

Spiritual Comfort

Eliminate Illusion

A step-by-step contemplative exercise that will help to liberate the participants from illusion and open their eyes to the glory of the Sea of Love and Mercy awaiting them

Here is an effective spiritual exercise by which to visit Sugmad daily:

1. With eyes closed in a comfortably seated position, sing your secret word or *"HU"* or *"SUGMAD I AM COMING."*

2. Envision yourself standing in the River of God as it pours forth out of the heavens above.

3. You may ask for the presence of your current or favorite guide or teacher or Dan Rin. The River of God consists of molecules of white and gold Light and Sound, which look like a torrent of water but feel as light and uplifting as God's loving breath.

4. Feel the River of God's loving Light and Sound focus on you and wash over you, carrying away all doubts, fears, anger, attachments, and any other obstacles that remain between you and Sugmad.

5. Let yourself be washed clean inside and out.

6. Smile in your purification with joy and absorb the miracle of this moment.

7. The Master may come and ask for a sacrifice. He or she may ask for your heart. Give it without hesitation. Be willing to sacrifice yourself – you will never regret it.

8. Feel yourself moving upward toward the source of the river and move out of the flow and into the higher realms beyond the mind.

9. Feel and intend to move into Sugmad's realm.

10. Ask for guidance if you choose, but also trust that you know the way home, even if you do not remember. Building upon past experiences, feel each world, dimension, or plane as you pass through, never stopping no matter how great the love, and Light and Sound you encounter.

11. Keep moving toward and opening to Sugmad, singing your secret word, "*HU*," or "*SUGMAD I AM COMING*" inwardly with great joy and anticipation.

12. Keep opening until you know that you have arrived. You are an invited guest.

13. Speak or do not speak, as you wish. This is your home and you are welcome in it.

Spiritual Comfort

Thank you for listening to what I have to say. If you would like further instruction or presence with me, simply make an appointment with my assistants. I teach in Ekere Tere. You are always invited to learn and share your wisdom.

~Master Quetzacoatl

Experience the Soul Plane and Beyond

Only those with pure hearts and intent should try this powerful technique, for, if misused, it will cause serious and immediate harm. If used as directed herein, it can substantially raise the vibratory rate of the contemplator and propel him or her into the higher, Inner Worlds. It can be combined with spiritual exercises of the heart, as taught by Dan Rin, to propel the consciousness of Soul into the Soul Plane and beyond.

1. First, you will need to contemplate the form of the star tetrahedron, a 3-dimentional form that represents a perfect intersection of two tetrahedrons. A tetrahedron shows perfect equality of the power of 3 – it is the intersection of three equilateral planes – all angles and length of sides are the same. It is best if you have a small model at hand. It can be simply made out of card stock with scissors and invisible tape. Each star tetrahedron used in the Merkaba technique is in proportion to the individual's body. It is

essentially an imaginary form tailored to your size.

2. Here is the new Merkaba technique: Focus on your heart and say, *"All I send out in Divine Love comes back one thousand fold. I send only love and ask to come into the Light and Sound of Sugmad."* Sing the mantra, *"MER-KAH-BAH-LA-HU."*

3. Imagine you are sitting inside a large star tetrahedron whose top point extends to an arm's length with fingers extended above your head. The bottom point would be an arm's length below the level of your feet. The forward and rear points rest at the level of your heart, again about arm's length with fingers extended.

4. Sit comfortably within the imagined shape of your personal star tetrahedron. Sing the mantra above. Get a clear sense of each tetrahedron as separate. Start each one spinning in the opposite direction – one spins to the left and the other to the right. You may start each separately to get a clear sense of it spinning before beginning the other. It does not matter which one spins first. Begin the spin slowly for the first few times you try this, to adjust to the increased vibration it creates. Spin the tetrahedrons more rapidly as you feel comfortable until they spin at the speed of light and you are

lifted out of the body. You may see the energy field around you expanding to a minimum of 55 feet in diameter.

5. Remain focused in your neutral center with your heart open wide to Sugmad's Love.

6. Take it easy with this exercise. It is very powerful. Adjust to it slowly so you do not get out of balance and become ill.

~Sri Kadmon

Find your Daily Direction as Soul

A contemplative exercise that will enable the practitioner to listen to the direction of their own Soul

1. Settle into the quietude of contemplation with the *"HU"* song and your sacred word.

2. Bring your focus on the Eyes of Soul looking into the heart of Sugmad and see the swirl of colors that are its vibrations of love. There will be some of these colors that will harmonically resonate within your Heart Center.

3. As you come out of contemplation, take pen and paper and write the question: *"What is my direction as Soul today?"*

4. Use the mantra *"MUTA-PARUM"* spoken <u>three times</u> slowly; this will translate the pure transmissions of love into useable directions as you begin to write.

~Babaji

Gain the Presence and Protection of the Inner Master

A contemplative exercise that aligns the participant's consciousness with the protection and presence of the Inner and Outer Master

As with all multi-layered spiritual exercises, you may complete one step at a time, then open your eyes to read the next step and practice that step until mastered, then read the next step and practice it, and so forth.

Practice this exercise alone in a quiet room in a comfortable position several times to get a full opening of consciousness and connection. Then after you have been able to do it in full while alone, try doing this exercise in silence while on a gentle walk around your neighborhood, in the market, in your place of employment, or seated at your family dinner table.

1. Sit and relax in quiet contemplation, singing your choice of your secret word, name of beloved spiritual guide, or "*HU.*"

2. Gently place your attention in your Heart Center and feel its warm pulsing. Send your heart a prayer of gratitude for working non-stop while you go about your day and while you sleep. See your heart slowly and gratefully open as a pure white thousand-petal lotus reflecting the radiant eternal sun of Sugmad. See the light within your heart radiate out in all directions.

3. Sing the following mantra as a love song: "*SE-HA-JI-DAN-RIN-ME.*"

4. Ask the Living Sehaji Master as the Inner Master, to meet and align with you to guide, protect, and bless you with Its Radiant Presence.

5. Feel the center of Light, Sound, and Unconditional Divine Love of the Master's radiant heart align with your heart. Feel the pulse of energy flowing white, rose-colored, and golden; sparkling back and forth between your smaller heart and Its much larger heart. Feel the protection of Its presence, ever beating, pulsing, and flowing with Light, Sound, and Unconditional Divine Love. Feel free to modulate the intensity in small

increments. Stay in this bliss as long as the experience lasts.

6. Upon your return to your human consciousness, give a blessing of thanks to the Inner Master.

7. Practice Its presence and feel Its protection for the rest of the day.

~Sri Rama

Glimpse God-Realization

A contemplative technique that will give the participant a glimpse of God-Realization

1. Go into quiet contemplation and ask the Inner Master for a glimpse of God- Realization. Quietly within your own heart, envision a golden white light glowing, gaining in strength and momentum, flying out in all directions with the strength and force of a mother's love for her child.

2. Sing *"HU-ALAYHA"* for a few moments. You are a child of Sugmad.

3. Envision and feel the more powerful love of God, your parent, gently connecting to your heart, and as you rejoin in full consciousness, thank the God who gives you continual life for the blessings bestowed upon you each day. Bless all inside you, all outside you, as you and God merge into an infinite golden globe of universal absorption.

~Dan Rin

The Importance of Self-Realization

A contemplative technique that will give the God seeker a deeper insight into Self-Realization and its importance to spiritual unfoldment

1. Formulate a true and precise question to ask the Inner Master to gain a deeper insight into Self-Realization and its importance to spiritual unfoldment, as the true yearning of your heart and soul.

2. Write the question on the top of the paper, then close your eyes and sing *"HU"* five times.

3. Sing *"HU-LA-MAYTA"* three times and *"HU"* five more times.

4. Then ask your question again, as you envision meeting the Inner Master or your own soul and Oversoul in their radiant bodies.

5. Hold your vision and know this is manifesting as you are creating it within the vision of God that is in you.

6. Focus on your Heart Center connecting to the heart of God and go deeper into the opening that will follow.

7. If a clear answer does not come, do the exercise daily for seven days, changing and refining the question or techniques as is needed for your true and unique self. Know that the answers to the question you have asked lie within you.

Feel free to refine the question, as you feel nudged to do. Know that as you ask, so you shall receive!

~Dan Rin

Grow your Spiritual Awareness

How Universal Soul Movement expands the spiritual consciousness of the practitioner

The rate of transformation in the Souls of this universe has been put in a very delicate balance and is supported by the energy brought from other parts of this universe. As the awareness of Soul grows in the participants of The Way of Truth, each of you have the responsibility in your Universal Soul Movements to bring certain information to the Living Master as he is guiding you through the karmic duties in the time of change and growth. In order to be the vessel of knowledge that is being sent to this universe, the practice of Universal Soul Movement is essential to maintain the flow of the Light and Sound. As your heart begins to sense its true, selfless nature as Soul, the vibration of the love of Sugmad that pours through your consciousness is raised to higher levels. It begins to prepare you for your travels in the God Worlds as you move toward mastership in the Great Sea of Love and Mercy. In times to come, you as Soul will navigate this plane of existence as the captains of your own destiny in your usefulness to the Love of Sugmad to many other beings. In the form of Spirit, Soul is the greatest messenger of Love to other beings that will be encountered as the mission of this Sugmad is fulfilled. You shall, in your own growth, see what the true meaning of the transparent, selfless heart carries to those that wait in other realms of beingness, as The Way of Truth is destined to bring the message of Sugmad's Love to them.

~Sri Kadmon

Open to More Wisdom

A contemplative exercise constructed to open the doors of greater wisdom for the participant

This is an exercise of simple beingness in the moment where all wisdom exists. Wisdom is experienced before the Mental Body can intervene on the conversation between the selfless nature of the heart and the connective vibration of soul to the knowledge within Sugmad's heart from where all wisdom is born.

1. Settle into your contemplation using the name of God, which can be found with your heart during the minds most quiet moments; listen carefully for it.

2. Speak it inwardly three times.

3. If you are unable to access its use, then *"HU"* five times and allow silence to ensue.

4. After a few moments, you'll sense the stillness of the Mental Body and your consciousness will cross the Etheric Plane into Soul Awareness.

5. Then say these words: *"NASTRON-DEU-TRA-NASTE."* Using the mantra will focus Soul into the single moment of all wisdom.

Spiritual Comfort

6. Be prepared for sudden feelings of tremendous openness like a sudden light shining into a great darkness and revealing everything that is beyond sight in the form of nothingness, and within this vibration you shall find the true essence of wisdom.

~Babaji

The Quickest Way to God

The Middle Eye is the gateway for the vision of truth and the Inner Worlds of God, and it is keyed and locked to prevent the opening and vision of those who are not yet ready to see; and so, when HU is sung and the spiritual exercises practiced, the subtle bodies are refined and removed of dross and impurities, and man is brought to a greater level of understanding and closer to the goal. Once a sufficient level of maturity and awareness is reached, then, the Spiritual Eye shall open in a timely and normal way, to further aid the student along his path and return home. The singing of HU and the spiritual exercises are the fastest way to clear the bodies and quickly move to that place that the student is ready to have his [or her] Eye opened and see the mysterious glories of God.

~Sri Leytor

Take Your Next Step to God-Realization

What I would say to the God seekers of today to inspire them to take that next step to God-Realization

There is only God. All live in God, but all know it not. Only you hold the lever to open the door to God in this very moment.

1. Live and move, breathe in and feel God rushing through your veins like the blood that gives you life.

2. Say your prayer of vision and gratitude every time you pause.

3. Reconnect and do it frequently throughout your day and night, even when you roll over in your bed. Imagine it to be and it is.

4. Devise your own or say the following, as a reminder and a sacrament: *"Dearest Sugmad, Great and Eternal Truth, you are the One in whom I live and love and have my very being. I breathe in your fragrant breath and bathe in your loving sweetness. Purify every part of me to enrich the fertile resonance of my soul and plant your seeds of courage, freedom, and everlasting love. Flood my soul and all my bodies with your Divine Grace. Infuse in every cell of my entire being your*

Spiritual Comfort

Loving Grace so thoroughly that I may shine as a testament of your great love and give nourishment to every soul I encounter throughout my day. Where there is not love, let me sow love. May I shine and water the garden of my life with your Everlasting Love and Wisdom flowing though me. Shine brightly within me so that I may share in the healing of my fellow travelers, whatever their origin or present state of being. Let me be a light in the darkness so that others can find their way home to you, too. In gratitude for your Grace, I devote my every thought and deed to you. Blessed Be."

~Master Parmenides

Working towards God-Realization

♥ Overcome feeling stuck by your own impurity

♥ Embrace transformation and acceptance

The Tumultuous Ocean Cleansing Technique

1. Imagine yourself in the Higher Worlds of Sugmad. Ahead of you are the falls of the Big Gold River. This river runs tumultuously among rocks and falls several miles below – it is like a big torrent.

Above the river is a red sun just like what astronauts call "a big red."

2. Imagine that you are getting into the river where the falls start. You are the same substance with that river; you melt into it and yet maintain awareness of your own self as you now cascade over the falls.

3. It bounces you back and forth, side to side, and all fears and impurity are washed out of you. The falling is to overcome your fears – it is a *sine qua non* condition to get into the superior part of the Higher Worlds.

4. You leave the river and fly to the big red sun and enter its heart; it welcomes you with such warmth that you turn pure gold. This is the Sugmad accepting you now as the return of one of Its children. That will open the door to know more about God Consciousness.

~Dan Rin

Spiritual Comfort

Understand the Truth in any Situation

Here follows a spiritual exercise that will develop the soul's ability to intuit the truth in personal matters and events

1. Imagine you are sitting before a full-length mirror with a clear view of yourself. See that a light is shining over your head; it is golden with deep orange tones.

2. Allow yourself to float into this light and become one with its warm, pulsing energy. This is the light of your own awareness and ability to discern the truth behind all the events in your life.

3. Keep watching your image bathed in this light as you sit in front of your Inner mirror and chant this mantra three times: *"RAY-SO-LA-TE-MAY-TO"* (pronounced "ray so lah tay may toe.")

4. Now call forth one of the Masters of the Sehaji with whom you feel a close rapport and ask him or her to show you an image of the truth behind any person, event, or situation in your life that you wish to understand. Ask your question and then keep your Inner eyes focused on your mirror and watch as it clouds over with mist. After a few minutes the mist begins to clear and you will see an image slowly come into focus. It may be a

literal answer to your question, or it may be something symbolic for you to interpret with your Master Teacher. You may also get a word or sentence or even a story about your question. This may come now or at a later time when you are busy with your daily activities or when you are resting. When it comes, write it down in your journal. If you do not understand the answer to your question, take it into contemplation and ask for clarification. Your truth will be made known to you. Blessed be.

~Dan Rin

Spiritual Comfort

Chapter Five

God-Realization and Giving Love

Spiritual Comfort

The High Road to God

As you see the road to God-Realization stretched long and desolate before you, do not look from start to finish, and do not even look one step ahead, but watch your feet that move effortlessly by your love for Sugmad (God) and all that is within Its Mercy. It is your love for God that will move you forward and nothing else. There is no goal greater than that, to love and understand God. How do you keep love in your heart when there is nothing but darkness around you? By blessing all that you encounter in your day, no matter what it is, bless it and watch the road disappear under your flying feet. This is how the Wise Ones completed their long and winding journeys -- by seeing nothing but the face of love in all that they encountered. They did not look at the tiger's fangs but saw the grace of its movements and the beauty of its fighting spirit. They blessed its ability to tear them apart and honored the divine source of the power behind it. In this act of love, all tigers of the world bowed before them and let them pass unharmed. You can walk through the valley of darkness and wild beasts and see only the flicker of moonlight bouncing off a leaf. Keep your eyes on that spot of light; acknowledge only love and all dark and savage things will retreat from your path.

Herein follows a contemplative exercise to journey with Master Rebazar Tarz to his abode in the Himalayas for conversation and enlightenment:

1. Imagine yourself in sturdy hiking clothes and standing at the feet of the Himalayan mountains high in Tibet.

2. A guide approaches you with a llama in tow; climb aboard the llama and allow the guide to gently lead you on the path up the mountainside. It is a sunny and warm day and the sky is a deep, azure blue.

3. Breathe in the clean air and enjoy the feeling of going higher up the mountain of your consciousness. Presently, you can see the round dome of a white hut at the top of the trail and as you get closer, you can see me standing outside waving to you. I appear many ways to many people and so it is up to you how you wish to see me. Perhaps, in my traditional maroon robe and sandals with black hair and beard, it does not matter; what matters is the love you will see shining in my face.

4. When you have my image clearly before you, say this mantra and the whole picture will become animated and "alive" - like a tapestry you can step into: *"RE-BA-ZAR-ALLA-TE."*

5. The rest of the contemplation is up to you; perhaps we are inside the hut having tea and conversation. Or perhaps I take your hand and we fly over the mountains to the God Worlds to visit a Temple of Wisdom. Or any number of scenarios that may be impressed upon you based on your needs and desires at the time. I am open to anything you need for your spiritual growth. Or simply say, **"Rebazar, take my hand and lead me where I most need to be at this time and tell me what I most need to know."**

Many blessings to the faithful, who seek the truth of God.

~Dan Rin

Align Your Self with God Consciousness

♥ Instructing Inner bodies to align with soul

"Inner talking" can be said and described as the practice of conversing and instructing the Inner bodies of man to constantly train and bring them into a state of coherence with the goals and wishes of Soul. It is the practice of affirming and describing what is the goal and method of operation, which each body should clearly see and understand what is expected of it to succeed in its mission and responsibilities. This does finally lead, as it is

successful, to greater levels of knowingness and beingness, as the Inner bodies do become aligned and coherent and the truth of Soul is able to penetrate and share the love and light of the pure worlds above the Great Divide.

To practice this means of unfoldment and the making of good progress, one must do the following:

1. Enter into quiet contemplation by using the secret word.

2. Then call to the Inner bodies and assemble them in front of you, and begin the dialogue and discussion to hear the thoughts and trials of each, and to instruct each in its duties and responsibilities and course of proper action.

3. And in this way will the Inner bodies learn and grow, and this Inner dialogue will be a powerful tool to aid you in your endeavors and struggles upon the path.

~Sri Leytor

Spiritual Comfort

♥ Aligning our consciousness with Sugmad

How we can align our consciousness with Sugmad on a moment-to-moment basis

To balance this Sugmad, it has been taught that only true acts of selfless love bring the joy that fills Its heart. To look at our actions through the eyes of Soul rather than that of ego and selfish pride, brings a higher vibration of devotion to caring for one another to our daily lives; that is, not to ask what it is that we need today, but what it is that we can give today through the selfless love that is bestowed so freely to each of us. The reason for the journey is to share the discovery of love and to show us at all times that this life is truly a gift that must be shared in all expressions of thoughtfulness towards those that we encounter still wandering in the illusion of pain and suffering; and therefore, to truly understand that God is the energy that drives every aspect of the Light and Sound seen through the eyes of the open heart in all beings encountered in this limited environment we call the physical. Our everyday duty to Sugmad is to share the knowledge of the heart and to show, through selfless acts of caring, the awareness that everyone is a part of the Light and Sound in this universe. You may travel on the Inner with the knowledge that, through your spiritual practices, all is granted to you from those planes of existence that you are privy to. Let the message of Self-Realization in Soul lead to the God energy manifesting in this day-to-day life.

Caring for one another is the grace of the true Soul that has aligned itself with Sugmad, again and again, throughout each day. It is the nourishment for this universe as it begins to open to its new beginning. Let the Light and Sound be felt in the simplest exchange of greeting. Let the heart of God be your only guide when you come to a crossroad of feelings. Let the light of your God Self shine on those moments of indecision that cause confusion on the causal and emotional planes, and always know that the Living Master of the Light and Sound watches over the outcome of all dilemmas you may face. Let your heart be touched by the hearts of others that have sought what you exchange with the Sugmad in your contemplations, so that they may find their way to the planes of true joy and love.

Remember it is the simple attitude of love that makes the greatest change in the outcomes of your day.

~Babaji

♥ Purifying and becoming one with Sugmad's consciousness

1. Close your eyes.

2. Gently put your attention onto the Third Eye.

3. Sing "*HU*" six times.

4. Sing "*Dan Rin*" seven times.

5. Begin to imagine within your Middle Eye a purifying golden light. It is morning and penetrating through your Heart Center and it is burning up all impurities completely. Feel the lightness that is coming through your body.

6. Repeat to your body so it understands and it works with the program, feel the lightness.

7. Chant the mantra three times *"SU-KI-LE"* (pronounced Soo-Key-Lay, which translates as meaning "I am one with Sugmad's consciousness; I am given the key to Sugmad.") three times - this represents the trinity of life. Feel the stirring in your Middle Eye.

8. See electric waves coming from Sugmad's heart, which is a pin point of energy in your Middle Eye, to the center of your heart and you may represent that heart as a flower.

9. You are seeing a ray of light hitting a flower that is your heart. You will feel a little jolt in your heart, and you will feel your whole being beginning to heat up. Your temperature is getting higher and love is filling your heart. As your body heat is getting hotter, energy cells of your body become alive and vibrate.

10. Sugmad is communicating with you. Now listen to your heart and listen to what Sugmad has to tell

you. Ask It to give you Its views of what is being conveyed.

11. Now you may slowly open your eyes and stay in the vibration of what has been awakened.

~Dan Rin

Developing More Love and Understanding for Life

A step-by-step contemplative exercise with a mantra that will develop more love and understanding for life

We have traveled outside this universe to bring back to you this powerful exercise to create an engram with your selfless heart that will grow in its intensity with each subsequent initiation. This will tune your ability to love with that of Sugmad; it gives you a clear vision of what to do to bring the true essence of the Light and Sound into every action of being, and how to do it. It will carry with it the information from another race of beings who have studied our evolution of love and wish to lend their findings to the re-awakening of love in all souls as they prepare to join with us once again. This is based on the tetrahedron design from Gopal Das.

1. As always, clear your mind of thoughts with <u>five</u> **HUs** and center your attention on opening the heart through the Third Eye consciousness.

2. The words *"QUA-SALTU"* will open the vortex.

3. Then <u>repeat three times each</u> of these words in three syllables:

    a. *"TE-NE-SIA*

    b. *"TE-NO-SIA" and*

    c. *"TE-NA-SIA."*

~Babaji

Loving in Balance with an Open Heart

Herein is a contemplative exercise that will give the participant a greater insight into how to give love in balance and with an OPEN HEART

It is in the many names of God that Soul can always find its way to the open heart and understand the need for balance in itself for receiving and giving through caring – a true selflessness.

This is an ancient chant to open the consciousness to balance through the many names of God. In this, to be brought across the universe to a sacred place where the true essence of balance exists in the heart of God, you may learn to give love in the greatest balance from within the open heart of selflessness: *"BRAHMAN-DAS-DEVA-SHIVA-SHAKTI."*

~Babaji

Prayer for Continuing toward God-Realization

An Inspirational Prayer for the God seeker to continue their journey to God-Realization

"Welcome, my brothers and sisters,
Welcome and heed my call.
I am the One God that lies deep within
The breast of one and all

With your eyes closed or open
Feel the deepest love you have known.
Imagine a duplicator at infinite light speed
Reproducing this love in all you have sown.

Pray with Me daily. Dance in Me gaily.
I am here whenever you call.

Spiritual Comfort

Sing HU loudly and other sounds proudly
For Life Everlasting is available to all.

Feel My Breath in your heart each moment
It is time for your turmoil to cease.
Through your clear and selfless heart and soul
May you ever know My Touch and My Peace."

Dear Ones, we love each and every one of you. Peace be with you.

~Master Mary Magdalene

Chapter Six

Utilizing the God Force in Your Every Day Life

Spiritual Comfort

Appreciating Beauty in Every Day Life

Opens God seeker's consciousness to the moment's beauty

The simplest way to understand the joy of love in life today is to be present.

1. In your morning contemplation request that you be focused through the selfless heart awareness of Soul as you walk through your day.

2. Always show caring for those you encounter in your daily travels and know in your heart that you are a messenger of Sugmad's love for all souls.

3. After <u>five</u> *HU's*, say inwardly three times: *"I am the embodiment of the highest laws of Sugmad."*

4. You may re-charge this energy any time during the day by simply repeating it inwardly.

~Babaji

Appreciating Life; Enjoying Living

How Universal Soul Movement brings a joy of living and an appreciation of all life to the heart of the participant

In the awareness of the Soul's process of unfoldment in this time through Universal Soul Movement, the selfless heart sees and feels the presence of Sugmad's Love in all transactions in the universe. Traveling these realms with the assistance of the Living Master affords the participants of The Way of Truth to return with the spark of the higher realms to which they have journeyed. As all things are changed by interaction with the Light and Sound, so it is when Soul touches the fabric of eternal existence during its journey to the infinite realms of beingness. When the selflessness of the Sacred Heart is touched, it translates into great joy and is transmitted to all other realms of existence, including those in the Lower Worlds of day-to-day living. How this is felt completely by the participant is in the heart exchange that takes place with all that come within the aura of the student. As the participant is drawn closer to the God Worlds during Universal Soul Movement, the intensity of the Light and Sound bathes travelers with the purest Love of Sugmad, leaving with them the overwhelming sense of well-being that is felt when held in the arms of Sugmad's Love for all.

~Sri Kadmon

Spiritual Comfort

Life's Challenges

Helps with questions about life's situations

1. Close your eyes, relax and slowly focus on your Middle Eye.

2. Sing *"HU"* five times and then allow quietude, and just let the pictures of the mind flow through your consciousness. The pictures represent Soul speaking to you through symbols.

3. After five minutes say, **"I operate from the heart consciousness of Sugmad,"** Inwardly or Outwardly three times, and then allow quietude. Soul will let you know when the contemplation is over.

4. End the exercise with the postulate, "Blessed Be." You have my love, blessings, and Darshan.

~ Dan Rin

Making the Right Choices

A contemplative exercise on refining spiritual insight into choosing the right job, career, and partner in life

1. Strip yourself of all illusion, disharmony, and doubt.

2. See yourself as nothing but soul, a huge radiant heart within an infinite, all-powerful love of the Highest and most creative God, Father of All. You are gifted with freedom, wisdom, love, and vision, an individual atom in the body of God.

3. Sing "*AL-SEN-TRO*" in multiples of three, to bridge the Great Divide, and ask to be shown what it is that you are looking for.

4. Let go of the mind and its old ruminations.

5. You may envision or see Dan Rin or me or some other Master and walk or fly with us for a while to receive the next part of the answer to the mystery you seek.

6. Repeat to gain more insight as often as you desire.

~Master Vasitreyas

Spiritual Comfort

Coping with Stress

A poem to read in time of stress and need — A gift from Sugmad

"O Sugmad

Allow me to rest my mind from its needs

Bring to my heart understanding

Let the eye of my Soul see the grace of your wisdom

in all that transpires

Let me give from the infinite Love that is my beginning

May compassion be the way of my thoughts

May forgiveness be the breadth of my feelings

Bring those not yet awakened to its peace and

give them rest from their fears

Let every effort of my being be that of infinite love

Let the day be that of the highest order of grace

And, O Sugmad, allow me to be like HU."

Dear Participants, I am and will always be with each of you. Thank you for your love, support and commitment to the spiritual mission of the Sugmad, Grand Council and the Living Sehaji Master.

~Dan Rin

Directions to World Leaders

How you can help the world now

Here are some of our directives given to world leaders, members of their staff, and the general population. If you do not know how to do any of them, put it in your action plan to learn how.

1. Do as Jesus recommended: Love God, love your self, and love your fellow human beings. Above all, act with love for God, for the greatest good, and for all humankind and all creatures of life upon the earth. Progress, not perfection, is the personal and collective goal, but never force or shame another into doing this.

2. Unconditional Divine Love for God, which could be the God of your understanding, is the number one goal for you and for all souls who wish to achieve God Consciousness. If you choose not to follow this directive at this time because other duties take up your time, then that is your choice. There is a time and place for everything. If it is not yet your time and place, it is fine.

3. Each person is responsible for his or her choices. Freedom is a right and a privilege given by God to all; freewill must be respected and honored even if it goes against your personal values. All humans have the right to work and fight for their freedom.

4. The name one chooses to call God Almighty - Sugmad, Allah, Jesus Christ, Buddha, the Great One - truly matters not. Freedom of religion, religious practice, and all actions taken in life as a result of the true tenets of one's religion are to be allowed, as long as it does not impinge upon the freedom of anyone else.

5. Every human being should have autonomy over their own body. A human chromosome, zygote, or fetus is of human material, but is not a person with rights until born. We encourage stem cell research from embryonic material; it is not against the will of God, any more than the many other ways humans interfere with natural life cycles. The right to choose what is to be done to one's body is one's right, and not for the government or others to dictate.

6. Each person is sovereign over his or her own self. Each has the right and duty to make his or her own choices. America is far from perfect, but the tenets of the founders were encouraged by the heavenly host to give each person freedom to

pursue life, liberty and the pursuit of happiness in any way they choose, unhampered by the preferences of those in authoritarian positions. The boundary of this freedom is not harming others.

7. Keep your promises and agreements. Your word is truly your bond in the eyes of the Lords of Karma, even if not in a court of law.

8. Do not trespass upon other people or their property. Obey the laws of human decency in all manner of interpersonal relationships, not just those that stand before the public eye. The eye of God sees all. The Angelic Host are around you all the time carrying out the will of the Great One. We know what you think, feel, and do.

9. Obey the spiritual laws if you want to be most effective. Learn what they are if you do not know. Books and teachings abound on these principles.

10. I did not add it as a directive, but acceptance, gratitude, laughter, and fun are the fruits of an open and loving heart that have made my path infinitely smoother, more powerful, more enjoyable, and more doable. By constant devotional acts, we create pathways to become vehicles for the Pure Love of God.

~Archangel Gabriel

Spiritual Comfort

The Eightfold Path

The Spiritual Master of olden days, Nairopa, gives you his greetings and gratitude for the work you do and has decided to release his Eightfold way to God-Realization to you this day. It has not been available to the students of the Light and Sound since the crucifixion of Jesus under the tutelage of Zadok. I am here to teach you the Eightfold Path. Many have understood it to be the Sixfold Path, and this is how I have taught it, but there are actually eight dimensions, and I will tell them now for the first time.

1. Love God with all your heart and soul. This must be extremely intentional.

2. Love your fellow man with pure joy. Allow yourself to see no evil in him.

3. Rid yourself of evil thoughts or thoughts that diminish or reduce others to less than Godly proportions.

4. Eat your food thoughtfully and carefully. (Small quantities are important. Do not overeat.)

5. Consume nothing that has its own consciousness. If you do, then its consciousness will meld into yours and interfere, most likely with steps 1-4.

6. Think of nothing but how you will serve others as God. (This will include your contemplations and meditations.)

7. Know that you as Soul are eternal, immortal, and ultimately indestructible.

8. See your body as nothing but a physical shell, but God's own temple, nevertheless.

~Master Nairopa

Develop Emotional Relationships

A contemplative exercise that will develop a longer lasting emotional, loving relationship

Make a time and place where you will be uninterrupted for at least one hour, for fullest benefit. Keep paper and pen or other recording device beside you, to capture inspirations and insights as they begin to come through. Pay attention to what you feel like, all by yourself. If any of the steps are hard for you, then just do one part for several days or until you can feel comfortable with it. Take as long as you need. Sometimes long and slow is best. Proceed with the next steps as you can - no hurry and make no comparisons with anyone else! This is for you *alone*.

Spiritual Comfort

1. Sink deeply into your body and your heart. Take some special time to simply feel the pulsing of your heart and inflow and outflow of your breath. Sense the movement of air on your skin and know that everything inside and outside of you wants for you to be happy and resting gently in the arms of the Great One. Tell your mind to take a walk in one of your favorite places and let it go until later. Do just this part until you feel your mind let go and heart open wide. If you feel emotions come up, honor them; allow them to be, and send them on vacation, too. If persistent, you can just gently feel them for a little while and allow them to move around inside your body, while paying attention without judgment, knowing you are safe and protected from harm. Then forgive and send unwanted emotions on their way, as separate energetic beings needing recognition and expression, not neglect, abuse, or death. Feel a shift. You are now feeling and sensing yourself as soul.

2. When in the soul awareness, imagine your heart as open as a many petaled lotus soaking up nourishing rays of the Great Light within.

3. Open your Inner ears to the Great Music of the Inner Planes. You may sing *AH-MAY-NOTIS-SENSE-AWARENESS* several times with tenderness and reverence.

4. Pay attention to details, to notes and tones. Hold gently, as with a velvet glove, to any soft impressions; stay with stronger experiences.

5. You may call upon me or your guardian angel or a spiritual master of your choice to be here and now with you. Ask to take the next step on a journey to a longer lasting emotional and loving relationship with the Great One, your own self, and with a partner of your heart's desire.

6. Be open in your heart awareness to receiving a great inflow of love from the higher realms to nourish you. This will prepare you to find anew the longer lasting emotional, loving relationship you seek.

7. Practice this exercise daily for two weeks or more, then move on to other things. Return periodically for a "tune up." Practice throughout your day loving yourself and loving what you do. If you do not love what you do, do something else and/or begin to put conscious love into what you do. In Avalon, we taught our spiritual aspirants to put 100% love and devotion into mundane tasks, into routines of hygiene, and every movement. We became love incarnate. When you practice this and can move in and out of this state of consciousness at will, you will love everything with a new clarity. Old relationships will take on a new

sparkle and room will be created for what you want and intend to have come into your life. The important part is attention to love in every moment, gratitude for what is, and surrender all that is not of the highest love. When you can achieve this state of consciousness and move back into it whenever you find yourself out of balance, you will attract all kinds of experiences you will find exhilarating.

8. Love all, forgive all, and honor all. This is true love and freedom. Practice until you cannot remember when you did not know how to do this. You will revolutionize your world. Without a word, life around you will respond.

~Master Ursula Pendragon

Cultivating Faith

How to cultivate faith? Ask Allah for the willingness to have faith. Surrender all control to Allah instead of trying to control what you feel and the outcomes of your actions. Get on your knees with your face in the dust, if you must, if that is what it takes for you to surrender control. That is not necessary for everyone.

1. Here is what is necessary: Trust the process of the internal spiritual realm becoming more real than

anything else. Your worldly, cultured mind may rebel but try it anyway.

2. Glorify Allah in your breath, your heartbeat, and the movement of energy in every cell in your body. See it; hear it; feel it; trust it! You must choose to glorify it. Glorify Allah in everything within yourself and outside of yourself, in the mysteries of the great cosmos stretching beyond the mind's ability to conceive. Glorify Allah in your neighbors, when the baby cries in the night, dogs bark and awaken you before you need to rise for work, and in the lowly clerks who get paid so little and take the abuse of so many. Glorify Allah in every blade of grass and weed in your garden, in every cockroach and snake, even though you would kill them to be rid of them in your home. Allah exists in all living and non-living things, in the consciousness therein, in the movement of the electrons and nucleus of every atom in creation. All are the essence of Allah. Glorify Allah in your prayers, in your meditations, in your walks among the pure growing things, in your spiritual exercises, in your ministry to others. Try it as an experiment for six months; watch the transformation of your attitude and your life.

~Archangel Gabriel

Harmonizing Your Life

Bring harmony and coherence to the Inner and Outer Worlds

A powerful technique and method:

1. Relate to all life and living as if only you and Sugmad existed and all that did transpire in your reality was a conversation and dialogue between you and It, as to your learning and unfoldment and the refinement of your perception and Inner abilities, for the goal in life perception is to see all in terms of balance and harmony and unity and wherever one does go to be the perfect expression of the love and God-power within the physical world. But to be this expression requires an eye and the ability to perceive at a refined level the fluctuations and tides of life.

2. And so, to refine this perception and hone this keen ability, the God-seeker should, in his daily affairs and duties, always cast an eye about with the hope and the intention of seeking the manifestations of the Sugmad within every person and object that comes across his path.

3. And with time and persistence, the seeker shall truly learn to see all with open eyes and perfect vision, for the truth it represents and the voice of

Sugmad unspoken within the physical realm, in perfect balance and harmony with all that It does touch and affect.

~Sri Leytor

Practicing Humility

♥ Loving yourself and striving to do your best

♥ Free yourself from The Dark Night of Soul and other human frailties

♥ Glorify God

Humility reminds us that we are not Allah. One must develop a deep sense of humility to develop and display pure divine love, devotion, and service to Allah and its creation and creatures, human and non-human. This keeps at bay the "Dark Night of Soul." Humility frees the stranglehold of attachment to results, greed, and desire for supremacy of the little self. Humility is the soap that cleanses the grime of daily living and washes from the Inner bodies' weaknesses and failings such as dishonesty, manipulative behavior, self-pity, disrespect, resentment, blaming, jealousy, slander, and judgmental intolerance. With humility, one can let go of an obsessive desire to control, and can soften, allow, and open gently and fully to a greater force than the mind can ordinarily conceive. With this softening and opening and relaxing, one can breathe deeply of this Great Life Force, of Allah.

One can sigh, *"Aaaaaaaaaahhhhhhhh laaaaahhhhh."* In breath and out breath, slow and steady: *"Aaaaaaaaaahhhhhhhh laaaaahhhhh."* One can begin to accept a much greater, vital, moment-to-moment, creative reality, pregnant with possibility, joy, patience, and loving-kindness.

Humility purifies, clarifies, and respects the generosity of Allah. Humility enables one to remember Allah in every moment and thus glorify His presence.

~Archangel Gabriel

Develop Spiritual Intuition

A contemplative exercise that will develop spiritual intuition and perception

1. Sit tall.

2. Open your heart wide to God and your Third Eye in the middle of your forehead and sing, *"SU-RA-KA-SU, HU-SU."* Sing with all your love and ask for what you want.

3. Visualize the connection of these three and other chakras for better reception. Listen and receive. We will help you develop your spiritual intuition and perception.

~Master Kata Daki

Turn Negatives into Positives

A contemplative exercise that entails flat-lining the negativity out of personal obstacles by collapsing time and space

In order to turn negatives into positives, neutralize their effects, learn the most, and surrender all to Sugmad, you may do the following:

1. Clearly define your intention by asking - "What are my personal obstacles?" Write them down.

2. Access what you can about your personal obstacles and negativity about them. Use a journal to access and ventilate your conscious and unconscious emotional and mental debris in your Inner and Outer bodies. Take as long as you need; it could take several pages at least, maybe more, over the course of several hours or days, if you have never done something like this before. In

other words, learn what you can about your internal obstacles before attempting a Universal Soul Movement excursion. If you are mathematically oriented, then you may journal in mathematical symbols. Preparation is important.

3. You may want to use creative physical expression as well, in whatever form you enjoy or intuit would be useful. Pay attention to relationships between harmony, order, color, music, rhythms, form, feeling, and their relation to opening up more Light and Sound within your heart. Ask the Inner Master, "Do I really want to remove my personal obstacles? Am I willing to handle the corresponding changes it will bring into my life?" If yes, proceed.

4. Declare your devotion and mission to Sugmad, Dan Rin, and yourself.

5. With eyes closed, move your attention deeply inside your heart and sing: *"DAY-OH-DOM-IN-AY-OH."* Sing it 3, 6 or 9 times, in varying keys.

6. Envision yourself in a beautiful sacred space you have created or in a spiritual city you have visited or want to visit. Notice colors, music, rhythms, forms, and a pervasive harmonious feeling all around you and throughout all of your bodies. See new relationships forming, delighting your Inner

senses. You may converse with the Inner Master and the Light and Sound within your heart.

7. Explore nuances of your negativity to learn even more before letting it dissolve into the Holy River of God. Sense the infusion of purity of the highest realms and sense what changes may be needed for you to be in alignment with Sugmad's plan.

8. Return to your life knowing that the creation has begun. Sense the result as already present. Fold the future into right now. Continue to journal in words or symbols to capture the gross and subtle changes that come about in you day by day.

9. Let it go, and go on about your day without taking back any negativity. Should negativity arise, sacrifice it immediately and ceremoniously on the altar of the Holy Fire of Sugmad, using the mantra above. Trust the process. Observe the Law of Silence in telling others, but within your heart, know that what you have created is now forming on the Outer Planes.

10. The clearer you are, the faster will be your manifestation. Watch for results in a different form than expected. You will bring what you create, but Sugmad's gift will add even more. You may repeat this exercise no more than three times per

week over the next six weeks, if you sense and agree with the Inner Master that it is needed.

11. The use of the creative imagination, envisioning your unity with your desired creation, complete and total immersion in the ever-present and ever powerful Light and Sound, and the delighted use of non-power are all as powerful as they are intoxicating. Enjoy!

12. There is one caveat. Creating in this way is powerful. What is created on the Inner will manifest.

~Master Pythagoras

Set Daily Priorities

Open yourself to Inner guidance

1. Start and end your day for the next week with the following: With an open loving heart and willing attitude, say the following as a reverent prayer/mantra: *"Show me thy ways, Sugmad. Lead and guide me to the best path for me to take in each moment today. Please help me set my priorities to best serve your will and bring me what I most want and need, for the good of all the people in my life, including me. I willingly and gratefully open my Inner and Outer eyes, ears, and*

heart to learn from my internal and external reality as it truly is, and not just as I perceive it. Allow me to maintain balance and objectivity as I grow to understand what it is you would like me to do."

2. Be sure to record the intuitive wisdom that will begin to be revealed and build upon it. Spirit and spiritual masters will make their presence and wisdom apparent. Capture what you receive, because no matter how real and strong your experiences will be, they can easily be lost.

3. Build on the positive memories Spirit gives you and disregard the rest with objectivity.

~Dan Rin

Attain True Reality Now

How to create what you want

1. At any time throughout the day, sing *"HU-SA-VA"* three times and say, *"I can create anything I want. I create love and peace in my heart in every moment, joy and fulfillment no matter what I do, wherever I am or whoever I am with. Please reveal truth and help me perceive accurately."*

2. Focus on Sugmad is what counts and gives the energetic confirmation needed to align with the highest laws and intent of the Great One.

~Dan Rin

Spiritual Comfort

Understanding the Hearts of Others

- ♥ Give greater love to others
- ♥ Help open your heart

Father, Make Me More Like You

"Father, help me to see the light that shines in the heart
Of every soul I encounter throughout my day.
Help me to smile
Into their eyes when there is no kindness or
warmth reflected there,
And let me be the one who offers the gift
of compassion and mercy.

This is the time of true Brotherhood on Earth when all souls
Seeking redemption can come together and
find real understanding
In our brother's and sister's hearts by
stopping to listen to each other
And truly hear what each one has to say.

To **listen with love** is the forgotten art that
brings color and beauty
To the tapestry of life; it is what makes a
palette of grays and blues
Explode into a canvas of brilliant flowers
bathed in sunlight.
Help me listen to my brethren and truly give of
my attention and love.

The **world will open its heart to me** when I
am opened to the world.
There is **no need for loneliness and despair** if
I will but take the hand
Of the one who is lying in the road and
gently help them to their feet.
Then together we can find the sun that lights
the greater path before us.

Nobody can do it alone in this earthly world; **we
came here together**
To learn to work in **harmony** with each other, and
be each other's cheerleaders

Spiritual Comfort

And comfort when the darkness falls so heavy on
our hearts. **Father**, let me find
The true center of love in every heart I encounter by
being a Magnet of **Thy Love.**

Before I go out each day, I will bless the morning and say, "**I give
and receive only love.**"
This will be the mantra that plays in my heart as I go
about my daily life,
And it will be what sings to the hearts of others and
will silently bless all
I encounter as a magnet of **love in the name of
the Father.**

In Thy Name, Blessed Be."

~Dan Rin

Feeling Well-being from Universal Soul Movement

How Universal Soul Movement brings a joy of living and an appreciation of all life to the heart of the participant

In the awareness of the Soul's process of unfoldment in this time through Universal Soul Movement, the selfless heart sees and feels the presence of Sugmad's Love in all transactions in the universe. Traveling these realms with the assistance of the Living Master affords the participants of The Way of Truth to return with the spark of the higher realms to which they have journeyed. As all things are changed by interaction with the Light and Sound, so it is when Soul touches the fabric of eternal existence during its journey to the infinite realms of beingness. When the selflessness of the Sacred Heart is touched, it translates into great joy and is transmitted to all other realms of existence, including those in the Lower Worlds of day-to-day living. How this is felt completely by the participant is in the heart exchange that takes place with all that come within the aura of the student. As the participant is drawn closer to the God Worlds during Universal Soul Movement, the intensity of the Light and Sound bathes travelers with the purest Love of Sugmad, leaving with them the overwhelming sense of well-being that is felt when held in the arms of Sugmad's Love for all.

~Sri Kadmon

Spiritual Comfort

Chapter Seven

Interpersonal Relationships

Develop the Law of Silence

A contemplative exercise which will develop the Law of Silence within the participant

Here is a contemplative exercise to connect to the place within Sugmad's heart that will become the repository of all you may not speak of, and a source of rejuvenation for having done the vital work of keeping the Law of Silence.

1. Go within to your most sacred and blessed place. Feel the rumblings of your heart and your body. Relax.

2. Shift your attention to Dan Rin. Sing "**O-DE-SAY-UM-MU.**"

3. Rise gently in a vortex of swirling golden light, through each successive higher realm, into the outskirts of Sugmad's Great Ocean of Love. Feel all that is not pure love and pure soul being washed away as you rise in consciousness through each realm.

4. View the penetrating Light of Sugmad's heart and ask permission to join your heart with Its immensity.

5. Join in the center of Sugmad. You are welcome here. You are safe here. You are loved here. This is your home, Beloved, to which you may return at

any time, as your pure loving self – Soul. You may hear music. This is the music to which all sounds go and from which all returns. You may stay here as long as you wish.

6. Return with a vow to only give this love of Sugmad to your family, neighbors, and "enemies." All that is not kind or loving must henceforth be given over to the music within the Sugmad. Breathe, live, and have your being in Sugmad, and know that all is well.

Observe the Law of Silence about your negative emotions, Inner spiritual experiences, secret word and initiations, and any other thing that might overwhelm or harm another person. You may place all these desires to share within this Heart Center of Sugmad each day. Walk in peace, love, and golden silence and know that you are God.

~Master Milati

Spiritual Comfort

Develop More Love and Compassion for Others

- ♥ Use your imagination to create a better life
- ♥ Trust God to lead you

Contemplation 1:

1. Take a deep and full breath, filling the lungs with air.

2. Visualize the soft sweet love Allah has for you, as your breath enters into your body and imbues you with radiance.

3. On the out breath, sing aloud or silently: **"AH-LA-HU."**

4. With each successive breath in and out, visualize, listen intently, and feel the love of Allah filling your lungs, moving as tiny powerful molecules throughout your entire body and being, into you and out repeatedly, into an energetic aura extending out farther and farther into the space around you.

5. Imagine Allah is controlling the strength of this exercise by what you need it to be.

6. Ask Allah to develop more love and compassion for others.

7. Ask to be entirely a channel for Allah's love and compassion energetically throughout the day, as you continue inhaling, filling, and exhaling.

8. Ask for balance; stay in balance.

9. Feel the unity and oneness; know it in your heart to be so.

10. Do this for as long or short as you wish, extending in time and space with each successive practice. For maximum benefit, you may work up to 20 minutes once or twice per day, for the next 2 weeks. You may do this at any moment you are challenged by another person's behavior or attitude.

11. Remember to do this before reacting in anger or fear. This is your discipline.

~Archangel Gabriel

♥ Develop surrender, humility, and unfettered love

Contemplation 2:

1. Sing "*HU*" six times, with gratitude and an open heart full of love.

2. Surrender to a feeling of increasing joy flowing from the heart of Sugmad to your own heart.

Humbly know you are but a servant to life, one who may ask for what you want and receive the blessings that help in Sugmad's will and ways.

3. Ask the Inner Masters to guide you to develop more love and compassion for others.

4. Sing: *"HU-RAY-TA-MAIN."*

5. Visualize great waves of HU.

6. Listen to the Great Current of Sound that can fill your Inner and Outer ears with song.

7. Imagine and feel Sugmad's love wash through your heart, mind, and all bodies, gently, as a warm shower or gentle rain, increasing your purity of love and focus on the Light and Sound vibrations as it moves through you.

8. See all impurities still inside any of your bodies, including emotions or thoughts of a social nature, flow out through your feet into the Earth, which can absorb and transmute all negativity into its fiery core without a shred of disruption to its mission. Let go!

9. Practice this cleansing daily, until you can visit and swim joyously in the great Sea of Love and Mercy that comprises Sugmad's heart. Remain open to Sugmad's subtle whispers in every

moment of your day or dreams, especially from others in your life, with gratitude and surrender.

~Dan Rin

Discerning the Truth

♥ Letting go of emotional turmoil

In order to discern truth within one's self and in others' words and actions, one must first let go of emotional turmoil. This is a discipline.

One must do whatever it takes to stop viewing through the lens of emotion, for your own emotions will color everything around you.

1. See, own, embrace, and let go of your own anger, sadness, pain, and strife, or you will not be able to discern the greater truth. In order to be aware of oneself as soul, a practitioner must learn to listen to the intuitive whisperings found within the Heart Center. When soul is awake and connected to another without the clanging of emotions, soul's truth detector will develop quickly, if used rightly and not ignored.

2. To live in reality, attend to your own filters of emotions and beliefs first.

~Dan Rin

Spiritual Comfort

♥ A contemplative exercise to further develop your ability to discern truth

1. Close your eyes. In contemplation, call upon Sugmad, Dan Rin, and/or a master of great merit, someone with whom you already have a loving connection.

2. Ask to be a loving vehicle for truth and love and to be able to discern truth from non-truth.

3. Imagine connecting heart-to-heart with the spiritual master and Sugmad.

4. Imagine all the love you have flowing out of you into the Great One and then flowing back into your heart with a tender sweetness, a loving light, a gentle music that brings tears of ecstasy.

5. Imagine it and an Inner door will open to it.

6. You may sing *"HU-TU-SAY-HU-GAK."* As long as you are within the open heart-to-heart connection, all non-truth will feel and sound hollow, or wrong, like striking a broken bell. This process is done by soul, not the mind. The mind lives in duality and by itself, cannot discern the difference.

~Dan Rin

Forgiveness

How to learn to let go and truly forgive – apart and with the person

♥ **A contemplative technique when apart:**

1. The first is to go in contemplation and call to the Inner Master.

2. Then in his presence, and with the imagined presence of the other, declare to the one who has caused you pain your heartfelt forgiveness and goodwill for the ignorant actions he did take to create the hurt you have felt.

3. Then, imagine the arms and blue light of the Master enveloping you both, as you honestly and deeply repeat this affirmation of forgiveness until the pain and hurt has completely dissipated and gone. Though this may take awhile, the pure light of love from the Master's heart shall aid to burn off any residual negativity and darkness within the Inner bodies and the karma that links you both.

♥ **When in the presence of the person:**

1. Another way to seek and find forgiveness is, when you are in the presence of the one who has hurt you and caused you pain, to in your Third Eye see

the image or blue light of the Master and in your heart repeat, "*I forgive you and love you as Soul.*"

2. And with the true and honest silent repetition of this affirmation, the hardness and negativity of the pain and hurt shall begin to fade and dissolve and the light of love shall be returned, and you shall be freed from the negative vibrations and karma that truly binds you to the other and the Wheel of 84.

~Sri Leytor

Measuring the True Intent of Another's Heart

To access the purity of another heart, listen to how many times they say "I" in their important conversations with you. When you first find a person whose presence sprinkles the seed of love, go into contemplation and use any mantra of choice. Then in contemplation visualize their face in your Middle Eye. Once their face is crystallized in your Middle Eye, then ask:

1. *"Are you here to collect a debt? "*

2. *"Are you here to pay back a debt?"*

3. *"Are you here for mutual love, respect, and true friendship?"*

Collection and the paying back of debts are in the mire of illusion, and both lead to highly-complex relationships. These complex relationships might be thick in intimate excitement but deep in karmic debt. The way of mutual love and true friendship is generally the way to go unless you need a spiritual lesson. The message from soul is generally clearer if this contemplation is done several times before any physical intimacy has occurred. Once the waters of soul have touched the scent of human passion, the voicing of soul will soften with the promise of what you want rather than what you are really receiving. In time, what is sweet can turn into a bitter, lukewarm burden of emotional regret and eventual pain.

~Dan Rin

Heighten the Vibration of Love

How to enhance the environment at home, work or at places of recreation

1. Instead of the usual sitting and relaxing and singing of HU, I would like the participant to pick up one of the books or discourses of the Way of Truth, it can be any one, and open to a page at random. Then focus on a line from that page, and read it silently or aloud to yourself. That will be the opening to this exercise.

2. Now imagine that you are sitting on a giant Ferris wheel, like the kind at an amusement park. Imagine you are at the top of the wheel with a view of the city you live in. You can see in all directions at once from your lofty vantage point. You can see your home, your work, and all your favorite places of recreation from here.

3. As you sit at atop the wheel, imagine invisible arms of light reaching out from your body and stretching over the entire city. Your arms encircle the places of your daily life. Simply imagine embracing them all at once like a mother holding her children close. As you do so, say this mantra three times: "*O-VA-MA-SU-LA-TE*" (pronounced "oh vah mah soo lah tay.")

4. Let the light of your spiritual embrace touch each place in your life – your home, work, etc. Take a moment to inwardly visit each place and say each time, "*I bless this environment with love.*"

5. Then stay in contemplation for the next 15 minutes enjoying the view at the top of your world. Blessed be.

~Dan Rin

Keeping Sexuality Sacred

It is truly an important thing for the student to keep his sexuality balanced and sacred to prevent of anything that shall create any ripples or residual effect that may later come to haunt him on the path, for the physical sexual connection to another is the way that can be made as a gateway and a channel for energy to pass between the two, and not all that comes with another is known or may be benign. To prevent the connection with dark energies and entities or other things unseen, it is important to keep the sexuality a sacred thing and space and act, that its intended purpose might be remembered and served to bring the student closer to the openness and love that is God's presence and loving light and truth that may be opened when the sacred space is remembered and created. Now, this is not to say that sex should only be reserved for marriage or done to procreate or prescribed by any other moral code that may be created and used by modern institutions to fulfill their will and ways and desires to have power over others of their flock. This is only to say that sex should be reserved and engaged in within a sacred space that reflects the sanctity and nature and divine manifestation that it does represent and can be used to achieve.

And so, to keep the sexuality sacred the following can be used and done, that the student shall be protected from any unseen harm and way.

1. When the intimacy of the two does draw near, the student can, in his or her imagination, sing the sacred *"HU"* five times and imagine the two lovers surrounded by the blue light of the Living Sehaji Master and protected by his love and the truth and purity that he does represent and give.

2. The second way is, if both lovers are participants in The Way of Truth, or open to the practice, to together sing the *"HU"* five times before the loving is begun, and declare together the presence of the Master to protect and watch over you and bring the sacred love and power of the Holy Spirit within the embrace you share.

3. The third way that may be utilized is, before the night is begun, to sit alone in quiet contemplation and with a heart of love declare yourself a vehicle and channel for the Sugmad, and that whatever does transpire between you and any other is the work of the Sugmad and you will faithfully proceed and, with a heart of trust, shall create a space of love and safety for the one with which you do find yourself near.

And by using any or all of these techniques above shall the sanctity of the sexuality and its power be preserved and protected from unseen forces that may seek to do you harm or impede your progress on the path.

~Sri Leytor

Attracting the Proper Life Partner

We, the Sehaji, understand the difficulties that some of you, as God seekers, may experience in finding emotional balance through a life partner. I wanted to add this contemplation here for those who require assistance in this area of life.

A technique for the God seeker to bring the right, compatible person to them for their spiritual lifestyle

1. Define what you are looking for.

2. Set your intention to find it. Ask for Inner guidance to find the person on the Inner Planes first and make the connection. Begin a conversation and find out your reason for being together. If it is in alignment with the wishes of Sugmad, is for mutual love, and works toward your mutual goals, the relationship will be able to flourish.

3. Answer two questions: What are you willing to give in return for manifesting this relationship? What are you not willing to give in return?

4. Let go of fears. Of course, the first step here is to identify what those fears may be that hold you back from allowing, welcoming, embracing, and fully loving the person you wish to bring into your life.

5. Invite this person to come into your life now. Do not allow yourself to be discouraged when feelings come up. Focus on the Inner relationship to work out any kinks or barriers.

6. Let go of the desire to have a mate and go about your daily business. Work with confidence toward achieving your goals on all levels of your life, with the central position of Unconditional Divine Love for all life and devotion to the Great One.

A few words of warning: This exercise must be done soul-to-soul as a general invitation. Do not conjure up or try to manipulate or change anyone on the Inner Planes, as that would constitute black magic, would impinge upon another person's freedom of choice, and boomerang back on you with a vengeance. This exercise must be done by giving the utmost love, freedom, and sincerity - the same spiritual freedom that all participants in The Way of Truth are striving toward.

The Father of ALL is the Ultimate Freedom. Though FATHER is neither male nor female, the use of this term is simply my term of endearment and love for IT. His imperative is to allow all souls complete freedom to make their own choices, even if it means they will hurt themselves, but will not necessarily be able to hurt another. To hurt another is a violation of spiritual law. When Soul has awakened to the call of the Light and Sound of Sugmad, it strives to move ever more into the heart of Sugmad. After dwelling there for some time and serving in the spiritual hierarchy, Soul may hear the call of the Great Father Beyond this Sugmad, and be granted permission to venture further. For now, I will limit this discussion to within the realms of this Sugmad, which is enough of a goal for most of the participants of The Way of Truth.

The spiritual freedom you are seeking is to expand the heart consciousness beyond former restraints, fears, and false limitations, and to set sail for adventures in the great realms beyond your former experience and understanding. You desire to make your own choices and grow into the fullness of who you are meant to be. The participants of The Way of Truth are the archetypes of the sons and daughters of God. You have more freedom than you know what to do with. To learn how to fully activate Soul, to move beyond the confines of your emotional and mental programming, to embrace the unknown with joy and exuberance heretofore not exhibited, to go beyond your wildest dreams - all this awaits you!

~Sri Leytor

Spiritual Comfort

Manifesting a Life Partner – for Females

For the female participant in The Way of Truth who seeks to manifest a mate in a balanced and neutral way, the following technique may be utilized, although it must be understood that given the underlying dynamics already mentioned, and the role of human will, success may require great discipline and commitment to the path and the exercise that is given and shared. And even then, it may take some time to finally achieve the desires of your heart. To manifest the one you do desire, you may do the following technique.

1. When in quiet contemplation with the secret word or **HU**, gently see the Master standing in front of you or as the blue light of his love and protection and grace.

2. Then, in the light, put yourself in a chair seated and facing him and next to you another empty chair shall you place and tell the Master humbly, with a heart full of love and hope, "Master, please fill this chair with the man who is spiritually compatible with me and who will serve the highest spiritual good of all concerned."

3. And with repeated practice you shall finally find the one within your life who is a good fit and match to yourself and the goals of your two lives, and in this way may you enjoy a life of satisfaction

and harmony in the arms of a beloved one who will join you on the path.

~Sri Leytor

Parenting – Helping Children Survive Spiritually

A contemplative exercise that will give parents skills to develop the necessary levels of introspection within their children, in order for them to survive as spiritually balanced beings in this life

1. Sit with your children held in the golden light of your selfless beingness.

2. Bring into your awareness the complete love of Sugmad's heart to protect and cherish them as you do.

3. Holding this consciousness, begin a **HU** song and continue for as long as you wish. During the **HU**, see the golden light gently hold them and see it being absorbed into the center of their souls. Within this golden light, infuse the path of the Sacred Heart to unfold in their lives at each juncture of change and/or moments of confusion.

4. At the end of your *HU*, to safeguard and insure its activation, use this Ancient Egyptian mantra: *"TUTRA-TETRAN-TOLTE."*

~Babaji

Resolving Personal Problems

A contemplative technique with a mantra that will develop a deeper use of the participant's skills to resolve personal problems

1. Sing *"HU"* six times, with gratitude and an open heart full of love.

2. See, hear, and feel joy flow from the Heart of Sugmad to your own heart and out into the room or location where you are and then out into the world.

3. See, hear, and feel soul dancing lightly and joyfully on these expanding, colorful, harmonious waves of love, simultaneously out into the world and deeper into the Inner Worlds into the higher realms. Soul's focus may be larger than the universe or smaller than an atom. As soul, there are no limits to where you may place your attention and receive knowledge and wisdom. All the Inner and Outer Worlds are connected. Be the bridge; be the connection.

4. Ask Sugmad and one of the Masters to guide you to develop a deeper use of your skills to resolve your personal problems.

5. Sing: *"TU-SAY-TRE-TU-SAH, TU-SAY-TRE-TU-SAH MAY."* Obstacles will begin to dissolve on all levels in direct proportion with your measure of purity of love and focus of attention of utilizing the Light and Sound energies toward your mission.

6. Pay close attention and trust that whatever you experience is in accordance with your state of consciousness. Loving devotion to Sugmad's Best-Laid Plans will raise your level and states of consciousness.

7. Listen closely and make it so.

~Dan Rin

Seeing into the Hearts of Others - Scanning

This contemplative exercise will enable the participant to gain the insight and perception to look into the hearts of others.

The ongoing need for Soul to access the higher knowledge allows it to journey through the worlds of illusion without the cross connecting of karma with those who have not yet been released from the negative forces of retribution. When this overflow occurs, many souls suffer the causal setback that prevents them from gaining entry into the higher learning temples on the Etheric Plane. The message that each heart carries in connection to the karma it must process, is one of great value to aid the soul that wishes to continue toward God-Absorption. To see if understanding exists within the heart consciousness of another will help to keep a Soul of pure intent from being drawn away from the narrow path of purity and devotion by latent ego engrams. These obstructions manifest in the hearts of those who remain clouded to the illusions and the understandings that the Lords of Karma offer through the process of their lives.

To set the higher mental function into a scanning mode in order to detect a negative karmic influx, there has to be a recalibration to the Third Eye's sensitivity. This is coupled with an automatic spiritual shield reflecting back onto the heart that is clouded, with a stream of light. This reflection will illuminate to the consciousness that you are aware of its true intentions. You must remember that the key to any successful defense is the shield of Divine Love held with the heart of detachment and goodwill.

1. To set the higher mental function into a scanning mode, repeat this affirmation three times: **"I see**

from within, any vibration that will disrupt my karmic balance."

2. Then chant this mantra for three minutes: "**YU-SE-CIC-TU-TA-SE-NA.**" This mantra sets the pineal gland, which is the gland that governs the functions of the Inner vision on the Physical Plane, into an inverse rotation of the receptive energetic vibrations. This transmission will be sent to the heart, bypassing any mental involvement, allowing the heart to create the proper causal frequency to protect you from any karmic disruption.

~Dan Rin

Understanding People's Intentions

To discern the true intentions of those within your sphere, the following techniques may be used.

1. First, go in contemplation and within the Master's light see the face of the one in question and ask of him the truth of his intention and why he does come to you.

2. The second is, as well, in contemplation to speak to the one itself or its Oversoul and ask again the question of what is it that he does seek by coming into your reality and presence.

3. The third way that may be utilized is, when you are in the presence of the one, imagine you both within the light of the Master and silently sing three "**HUs**" and you shall receive a sign or intuition of what are the true desires and intentions of the one who comes to you.

Each of these techniques is equally powerful and valid. It is simply to the choice of the Self-Realized one to which he does prefer and wishes to use to aid him in his way and his endeavors.

~Sri Leytor

Understanding the Purpose of a Relationship

The relationships we do experience with all other Souls are of only three types and nature: One, to collect a debt that must be repaid from the other; two, to repay a debt that is owed by you to another; and three, for mutual love and support. However, this situation and truth is further confounded by the fact that relationships do have their own cycles and progression and a relationship may start as one condition and then with time and experience transform into another; and so, the key is always to be aware of what is the dynamic being enacted, to always know the proper course and action to be taken.

The impact this can yield on the relationship we seek to have can be this: If we do wish and desire to guide and develop each relationship into the karmically neutral and beneficial position of mutual love and support, then each interaction and connection must be given and held from that position within your own true heart, for in this way shall debts be paid and others be forgiven and the relationship can progress to the desired state.

There is as well, however, another technique which can be utilized to help to speed the progression to the desired end.

1. In contemplation you can go and seek of the Living Sehaji Master. Then in his presence, bring the other and have him or her stand with you within the light of the Master's love. And in this light say and declare, "*I have only detached goodwill and love for you, and I offer you payment for any debts owed, and I forgive any owed to me.*"

2. And with the repetition of this mantra and action over a period of days or weeks, the debt will be more quickly and painlessly paid and resolved without any actual action having to take place in the physical realm, or at least to a reduced degree.

And so, in this way can those relationships with others that do have some karmic root that requires resolution be quickly and efficiently dealt with and moved to the position of mutual love and support that always should be sought and desired.

~Sri Leytor

Chapter Eight

Finding Your Life's Mission and Spiritual Contract

Consciously Merging with Best-Laid Plans

A contemplation to learn the plan for your life

1. Imagine you are standing on a precipice gazing into a vast blue sky filled with stars. From out of the stars comes a bright sailing ship that flies through the air on invisible wings. It stops in front of you and you step onboard. The captain at the helm awaits you and can be any Spiritual Master of your choice.

2. And now you sail through the Inner realms until you see a Golden Temple of Wisdom in the far distance. As you approach it the Master of the temple comes out to greet you. This temple is Askleposis on the High Astral Plane and its Guardian is Gopal Das; this is where a section of the Best-Laid Plans of the Universe is stored and maintained. It is the section that is designated for the physical worlds.

3. Gopal takes your hand and leads you to the entrance of the building. As you step across the threshold, say this mantra three times: "*OLAY-VA-TU-MANA-TE.*"

4. There is a holy enclave that holds a gold-crested book containing the Sacred Plans which can be viewed as a hologram. The book is on a table in

front of an altar with two burning white candles on either side. There is a place to kneel in front of the book. Rest on your knees and simply ask to know the Plan for your life and how it can merge you with the plan for All Life. Ask to know your role in these holy plans of Sugmad. Stay in contemplation for as long as it feels right or until you have an answer. Many blessings are given you this day.

~Master Milarepa

Creating Your Mission

♥ Expand your creativity

Herein follows a contemplative exercise will expand the individual's creativity of his or her spiritual mission

1. Imagine what looks like a huge Sundial lying in the middle of a field of green grass on a sunny day. As you approach the Dial, you see it is divided into sections of service to mankind, such as teacher, healer, speaker, etc. There are many roles to choose from.

2. Walk to the center of the Dial and say this mantra three times: *"SULE-MANNA-RE-TA"* (pronounced sulay mannah ray tah.")

3. Now see where the sun places your shadow; what field of service is it in? You may have to do this exercise several times for the right field to reveal itself. This will stimulate your creativity as the many forms of service begin to reflect from your soul consciousness to your mind and appear on the Dial.

~Dan Rin

♥ How to feel and give Divine Love to the world

A universal contemplative exercise with a mantra that gives peace, love and brotherhood out to the world and to those of the open heart who seek spiritual comfort

1. Imagine in your Third Eye a large, soft blanket of pale blue, pink and lavender; these colors represent peace, love and brotherhood. With this covering you are safe in the arms of Divine Love and Mercy. Wrap yourself comfortably in this blanket and say this mantra three times: "*O-DE-SU-TA-LE-TO*" (pronounced "oh day soo tah lay toh.")

2. Now imagine a room full of people who are hovering in cold and in need of comfort. Go to the center of the room and place your blanket around them and see how it becomes large enough to

cover each person in the room with peace, love and comfort.

3. Say *"AH-DE-SU-TA-LE"* (pronounced as "ah day soo tah lay") three times and imagine the blanket now covering the entire world with the feeling of universal brotherhood.

4. Now simply enjoy the feeling of warmth and love as you share this space and time with your brothers and sisters.

5. Stay in this contemplation for 15 minutes and allow the blanket of peace to cover you all with the protection of God's loving grace. Blessed Be.

~Dan Rin

Increasing Your Capacities

A contemplative technique that will increase the intuitive and cognitive nature of the God seeker

1. With pen in hand, write your request for understanding upon the page to track and review later. Then sit with eyes lightly closed and gaze into your heart and imagine it shining and free of all previous bonds and limits.

2. Ask Dan Rin to assist and protect you. You may call upon me, if you choose.

3. Sing *"HU"* three times and then *"TU-VAY-HOOM"* three times.

4. Imagine standing on a mountaintop before the glory and magnificence of the Lord of all the worlds.

5. Imagine a strong yet soft and gentle light envelop your heart and open it to the whispers and secrets you wish to know. See your heart grow in size of consciousness. Send forth any fears or barriers that have kept it from being totally receptive to the calling of God.

6. Assume that you are moving in soul consciousness through all the planes until you stand in the plane in which you aim to go.

7. Feel the tenderness that Sugmad has for you, as part of Its own great Self. Feel and know that what you seek is being imparted to you now and will continue to be as long as you desire and remain open to receiving. Your mind need not understand or be able to put into words the information and experiences you receive. Tell your mind that you are safe and have indeed received the answers to which you seek.

8. When your Inner experience is complete, begin writing as if you are still connected to Sugmad through the heart and let any and all impressions flow freely without restraint or censure upon the page. Write until the flow stops, then ask for more and with eyes closed, reconnect as before.

9. Continue to work back and forth between your Inner connection and open eyed writing. Allow whatever comes through to come through. If you censor and stop the flow, you will not work through your fears and limits, should they arise. Nothing is foreign or unacceptable to Sugmad upon the written page. If what comes out shocks or disturbs you, then go within and ask to be shown what it really means. You have the power to destroy the written word if you so choose, but if you are not in immediate physical danger, then allow whatever you receive from the Inner to come through. You are developing courage, sensitivity, insight, and fortitude. Continue. This exercise is for you and will develop you as much as you allow. Blessed be.

~Master Senna

Spiritual Comfort

Inner Direction and Experiences

The relationship between contemplation and Universal Soul Movement

In contemplation comes the direction from the Living Master of the Light and Sound, Dan Rin, as to the purpose of your call to this way of life in The Way of Truth. The participants of this way of life have a very precise and well-defined mission, to bring the great love of Sugmad to all Souls that have been denied the warmth of Its immense power in their lives. The initiations that come are directed via the Inner awareness of the Living Master from the Great Ones that prepare you as Soul for your place in the higher realms of beingness. It is through contemplation that the necessary changes are made to karmic duties, the sensitivity to the new frequency of the Light and Sound and the ability to understand the knowledge that is being passed from entities of other origins than this universe, which sometimes are encountered during Universal Soul Movement.

The information needed to maintain the correct frequencies in the vortices that feed the healing energy to the Light and Sound anchored in certain places in this universe and on this planet has to be maintained as part of the karmic duties of the participants of The Way of Truth. Dan Rin has gone through extensive training to be able to manipulate the Light and Sound and is the one who has brought it to the peak of efficiency in this temporal reality for the initiates to use in their duties here. During contemplation the student

is trained by the Master to be of maximum use to this
Sugmad.

~Dan Rin

Illusion~ Techniques to Separate Illusion from Reality

The keys to understanding all that is seen and experienced
about the student in his reality in each day and moment in
time are the five different techniques, which do enable the
student to separate illusion from reality and truth and see
into the heart of what really is the matter and root cause of
all that does affect him.

1. The first technique and key is this, to softly sing
   HU in the imagination, in a quiet place, while the
   situation is pondered and the answer truly sought
   with an open heart and desire to know the proper
   course.

2. Second, to quietly ask for the Master whenever a
   situation does arise where the truth and proper
   action is difficult to discern and then watch for a
   subtle sign or key, as to the proper way and
   method to do what should be done.

3. Third, to see the words written in the imagination
   that describe the situation or question that one is
   faced with and concerned where you wish to find

a deeper understanding and perspective of what is the truth and way, and after the words are written on the Inner eye to see, the answer will be forthcoming in the hours or days to come.

4. Fourth, to ask the question while visualizing the Master and giving to his heart, the words of question and perplexity, which you do wish to see and understand, and know the proper course.

5. And fifth, and the most powerful technique for understanding is, in quiet contemplation, to go and place the entire situation within the blue light of pure love and God-power and ask to truly be shown the truth, as it may be and does exist in this time and situation with regard to the question you do have and wish to understand. And by using of these five keys and ways to understanding, the student shall never find himself perplexed or confused as to what is the truth or meaning or proper course to take when faced with the illusions or the other negative fields which do confound one's life.

~Sri Leytor

The techniques to separate Maya from Truth and come to proper decisions are these:

1. First, call to the Master in quiet contemplation until the mind does rest and you can begin to imagine the blue light. Then see the situation with which you are faced and see it enveloped slowly within the light as it dissolves and fades away. Then, ask the Inner Master to show you the truth of what is real, and in this way you shall receive a thought or image or impression or understanding of what is the truth of the matter. And for those less practiced in the art, you shall receive in a day or several a flash of thought and understanding, which does explain to you the truth you do desire.

2. Go into contemplation and see the Master's light, and then into the light, place the following words: *"Master, show me the truth in the area I now see illusion."* And in this way shall the Master bring to you the ability to discern the truth of the situation you do face.

Both of these are good techniques to see the truth within the illusion, and may be used by any level of student to aid him on his path and in his endeavors.

~Sri Leytor

Soul Contracts - Children's

Gives parents insight into their children's Soul Contracts

It was mentioned before that there may come a time when you may need to access the karmic and/or incarnation records of the child's Soul Contract. This request must be made of Kusulu for one to be offered an audience before the Red Dragon Order. To be granted this access, it takes the greatest effort of the selfless, detached, transparent posture of heart in Soul. As mentioned before, it is only in extreme cases that such a request may be considered, because the unfoldment of this universe is complex and may carry something beyond the understanding of the caring heart of a parent.

To make this request you must bring the support of the Living Master.

1. Go into contemplation using your sacred word, then call to Dan Rin to ask for an audience with Kusulu to take your request to the Red Dragon Order for consideration.

2. You will be asked to remain in the detached open heart consciousness so that there is complete clarity in viewing the scrolls.

3. The mantra *"SOL-TIG-NUM-SAT-LO"* was given to afford this consciousness in times of life

challenges. Say this mantra three times slowly at the end of the contemplation to afford spiritual protection to the child: *"TUTRA-TETRAN-TOLTE."*

4. This will insure the spiritual growth of your child with whatever the outcome may be.

~Babaji

Your Future

A contemplation to give insight into your potential future

1. The heart is an oasis from suffering and strife; imagine in your Third Eye that your heart is an island floating on a deep blue sea of possibilities and potential futures.

2. Sit down on the warm sand and write down a question about your future; it can be anything from asking about a romantic partner or a new job; or looking ten, twenty, thirty years ahead and more to ask for a window into the world to come and what will be your role in it. You can also ask about future lifetimes yet to be lived. Anything goes.

3. Write it down, then place the piece of paper in a clear glass bottle and toss it as far as you can into the sea. As the bottle leaves your hand, say this mantra: "*O-SE-TU-SAVA-TE*" (pronounced "oh say too sahvah tay.") It is only necessary to say it once.

4. Relax on the sand; lie on your back and watch the sky overhead. It is clear blue, but notice that wisps of clouds are forming in the center of the sky, making words and pictures. Just watch for the message they have for you in response to your question. It could be a single word, or a full length movie with color and sound. Again, anything goes. Experiment with this exercise and have fun!

~Dan Rin

Sri Kadmon and Your Life Contract

Love and work relationships

Sri Kadmon will work with you concerning your Soul Contract and past karma and will offer methods to improve your life. Your Soul Contract is the agreement you have made with the Lords of Karma. It is the agreement that guides your family situation, your monetary circumstances, jobs and career. This contract can be completely or partially changed under various circumstances unique to every participant of the Way of Truth.

This exercise can be used regarding people of all ways of life and life pursuits. You must trust what you receive and move onward with your life, not looking back.

Sri Kadmon offers a technique to give the participant true insight into the nature of their relationships in love and at work: When meeting a person for the first time, use this contemplation before any intimation and in-depth discourse begins:

1. Go into contemplation and sing the name of the Inner Master, Dan Rin, five times. Then visualize the face of the person in your Middle Eye.

2. Ask them if they are there in your life to collect a debt, pay a debt, or to give you mutual love and support.

3. If they are there to collect or pay off a debt, there will be a degree of pain and discomfort assigned to your relationship with these categories of souls. It is best to send these souls on their way by giving them your detached goodwill.

4. Once the first two categories of souls are identified, ask the Inner Master for the grace of having the karma connected with these people resolved and release you from having to continue

a relationship with them. Go into contemplation, visualize their faces in your Middle Eye and thereafter see the blue light of Spirit around them. Tell them the debt is resolved, to go their own way in detached goodwill. Once this contemplation is done, do not resume any further contact with this person. If you do, the Lords of Karma will presume you need the lesson with this person.

~Sri Kadmon

Your Spiritual Mission - Questions

Using contemplative exercises to answer questions

Each change in your initiation level may have an effect on the direction of your spiritual mission in life; it is necessary to maintain an ever vigilant awareness of the wishes of Sugmad in your daily life to understand Its needs for you.

1. Sitting in contemplation every morning and clarifying the heart so that it may receive the guidance of the Masters is the best method that I can offer for answering these questions.

The removal of ego from the actions of giving will align you with the highest wishes of Sugmad in your daily spiritual quest. The absence of ego makes way for the selfless nature of pure Soul to be available in all situations that may require the presence of the Light and Sound.

2. Singing the love song to God, the **HU**, inwardly <u>five times at four hour intervals</u> is a form of nourishment to the Soul through every day's journey.

~Babaji

Life's Concerns/Your Spiritual Mission - Insights

Part One:

A contemplative exercise with a mantra that heightens insight on areas of life concerns and one's life mission.

1. Write your concern or question on the top of a blank page.

2. Ask the Inner Master or God to show you now, or within three days, what is happening in greater depth in some area of your life concerns or life mission.

3. Talk to your mind, as if it were a trusted servant, and send it off in search of the answer. Ask aloud, on paper, and inwardly for help and surrender to what will come.

4. After singing "*HU*" five times, sing, "*Show me thy ways, Lord*" three times, and focus on your heart as the receptor for the answer to come through.

5. See curtains fall apart and truth rush in on waves of love, to be revealed a little at a time.

6. Upon opening your eyes, write your impressions under your question without mental interference.

7. For the next three days, watch for signs and intuitive images. For best results, always carry paper and pen to catch more. When your mind comes back to play havoc with your focus, send it off again, with love.

8. Repeat for three more days; review all clues and rewrite in new words what has been revealed.

~Dan Rin

Part Two:

(Do this technique after you have had at least several successes with the exercise immediately above.)

A contemplative technique that will give the God seeker the opportunity to see if there are segments of his or her Life Contract that can be changed.

1. Focus on your heart.

2. Sing *"HU"* softly several times and then sing *"ALA-SHANTU-AUM."*

3. Using Universal Soul Movement, see the garden and beautiful temple described above.

4. Meet with and ask Dan Rin and Shams whether segments of your Life Contract may be changed.

5. Open a dialogue. Honestly tell them what you want changed and why.

6. Listen carefully for their responses.

7. Remember that they are communicating with you whether their lips move or not, and whether you can consciously hear them or not.

8. Go with their guidance, stay focused and open, and record your experience, again for your eyes only.

~Dan Rin

Spiritual Comfort

Looking into Life Contracts and Prophetic Vision

A contemplative technique that will develop participants' ability to look deeply into their Life Contracts and the ability of prophetic vision to look within

First, you must commit yourself and necessary time to this undertaking, in all truth and sincerity of your heart's longing. Over the course of one to seven days, ask yourself several times each day what you really want to know about yourself and what you plan to do with that information. It will be very helpful to take walks in nature, especially into new settings that are beautiful and invigorating, to refresh many areas of your awareness. Write daily for at least five to twenty minutes on what is truly in your heart and mind. It would be helpful to consider this a sacred undertaking and use a fresh journal just for expanding this area of your life. Formulate, record, and number precise questions you want answered. Keep this journal and information to yourself! Allow what you already know to come up to conscious awareness. Pay attention to your thoughts throughout the day, Inner and other messages from your waking dreams of daily living, and dreams at night. Enter all into this journal, as answers will be contained therein. As you begin this process, dialogue with and keep open to the whisperings of the Holy One. You may do this while still performing other spiritual practices or contemplations. You will be transitioning and preparing yourself to take the next step that will help you to look deeply into your Life Contract and advance your ability of prophetic vision to gain the answers you seek. Design a resting place. Put aside other spiritual exercises for three days and focus on the one I will now share with you.

1. Sit in quiet contemplation where you will not be disturbed for at least 30 to 60 minutes, with the question of the day, pen, and journal ready.

2. With a clear and open transparent heart, call upon Dan Rin and one other spiritual master of your choosing.

3. Sing the words: "*FA-LA-NOL-TOR.*"

4. Imagine entering a familiar and exquisite Temple of Golden Light and Wisdom on the plane of your initiation, singing with the music of Sugmad. The air is fresh, clear, and cool and you are instantly filled with the warmth and safety of Sugmad's great and vibrant love. You are a Templar Knight come to claim the Grail on your mission of wholeness.

5. Enter a state of fusion with the consciousness of the masters and Sugmad, connected through the hearts of each.

6. Ask your question exactly as you have written it (only one at a time).

7. Listen with your heart to impressions.

8. Affirm a charter of truth and allow fictitious rumblings to be known as such, then fall away without further notice.

9. Write down immediately what happens when you come back into your room. If you do not think you have had any experience, then write as if you had, still in dialogue with the masters you are conversing with. Write "as if" and allow your experience to unfold through your intuition and whatever comes through without censure. It is vital to not censure yourself in your writing. You can re-read, edit, and see more clearly later. Allow an open flow between you as a multi-sensory vehicle and the masters and Sugmad as multidimensional transmitters. Trust what you get. There are gems contained therein with the answers you seek.

10. Continue to do this exercise for at least three days and up to as many as you wish. Return to it as often as you wish for further discoveries.

11. Contemplate your experiences for their treasures. Enjoy and Blessed Be!

~Master Brigit of Scotland

Reviewing Your Soul Records

A contemplative technique that will take the God seeker to the Causal Plane under Shams of Tabriz's direction to review his or her Soul Records

1. In a quiet safe place where you will be undisturbed for at least 30 to 60 minutes, settle into your body.

2. Breathe easily and focus on your Heart Center.

3. Ask the Living Master to guide you to the Causal Plane under Shams of Tabriz's direction to review your soul records. If you have a specific request in mind, write it down before beginning your Inner Soul Movement, and keep paper and pen close at hand to record your experience upon your safe return to your room.

4. Refocus on your heart and purest intention. Let go of any distractions.

5. Sing *"HU"* several times in a soft voice, and then sing *"SHO-TE-AUM."*

6. Focus on moving beyond the Astral Plane into the Inner Worlds and come to rest in a garden of great beauty.

7. Look around to experience the marvel of this place, and see a beautiful temple nearby. This is the place where memories of past and future lives are archived, called Akashic Records by many.

The great River of God (that looks to many like a huge waterfall rushing down from above) can be seen, bringing huge amounts of sparkling light, sound, and love into this plane from above.

8. Move up the stairs to the door of the golden temple building and meet the radiant master Shams.

9. He happily greets you and welcomes you into the temple.

10. As you move through the halls, notice the sights, sounds, feeling, and smells of this place.

11. You may be led to a room with books or screens, or simply move down long halls to see the answers to your query in the picture frames lining the walls or projected all around in holographic form. There are many ways to view your soul records.

12. Enjoy your experience; record it for your eyes only, and return for more experiences here as often as you feel called to do so.

~Dan Rin

Chapter Nine

Life in Transition

Spiritual Comfort

Beginning Your Day

♥ Discipline the Mind

A contemplative technique that will assist the God seeker in disciplining the mind

To bring the mind back from its wandering, takes a simple focusing technique each day to create the discipline necessary to keep a clear singleness of purpose. HU is the greatest multi-purpose focusing mantra. Sing *"HU"* <u>five times</u>, then settle into a brief contemplation and direct the mind to perform the duties of the day without concern to danger or mishap. Assure it of its protection by the love of the Inner Master.

~Babaji

♥ Protect your consciousness/space

The Grand Council is leading each of you to be in the God state of consciousness. Spiritual illumination means others will see your heart as the center of your being, and your eyes will be seen as God seeing through you.

1. Be active in your God Awareness and declare daily your home, job and family as "Holy Ground" by saying this declaration at the door of your home and workplace: ***"Let no thing, thought, nor being cross the bounds of my home, job and***

~ 178~

family, unless it is in accordance with the highest laws of Sugmad."

2.   Then sing "**HU**" three times and begin your day.

I do this exercise at my door every day. It keeps spiritual squatters and intruders from accosting your spiritual environment.

~Dan Rin

Environment/Surroundings

A spiritual mantra that will develop personal insights into the God seeker's immediate surroundings and environment

As I told a young lady this morning: Let your crown, mind, and throat open only to the Light and Sound and movement of the Holy Spirit as it moves you. Let no words of ego or power cross your loving lips. Let the day dawn over you and wash you in color splendid and never let a storm linger long enough to soak you to the bone again. Come out of the rain into the dawn at any time throughout the day, for it is ever radiant in God. Find it and go there. Live there for as long as you can and return as frequently as you wish. Stay present. Focus and live in the now. You may ask, "Show me thy ways, Lord," and sing the mantra: "*SING-ME-VA-HAIL-YA*."

Remember always - the heart is mightier than the sword.

~Dan Rin

Initiations

- ♥ Restore the power of your initiatory word
- ♥ What to do when your Secret Word loses its power

In some instances and occasions, the student's initiatory word can seem to run out of power and cease to function. This can occur for several reasons, however, the most common of which is that the mind has become aware of its usage and has moved to block its reach, and so retain of its own power and dominion. When this does truly occur and is experienced, several options do exist for the student.

1. The first is to go in contemplation and tell the Master of the situation and ask for his assistance to restore the power of the word.

2. The second is to go again in contemplation and ask that a new word be given, and then, if it is not immediately received, to watch the ebb and flow of daily living for the answer which will come.

~Sri Leytor

♥ Understanding your initiation

♥ Gain access and understanding of the abilities, scope and power of your initiation

1. In quiet contemplation, see the Master's face and blue light, and then to say to him humbly, "Master, when I am faced with difficult situations, when I would benefit from insight and the power of my initiation, please show these things to me."

2. And in this way, when the student is faced with some difficult situation or task or problem, then the Master shall aid in opening his heart and eyes to the solution that is available, to do what can be done and fully maximize the power of the circle and initiation.

~Sri Leytor

Law of Assumption

Using imagination to create what you want

It is a frustrating characteristic of the Physical Plane that this process does take more time to accomplish, for in the higher realms above the Great Divide it is an instantaneous process, however, such is the reality of this plane and the lessons it entails. The important rule and fact to remember, however, is that the prolonged and active and disciplined use of the imagination is the key to realization of the goals that are desired.

If it can be imagined and felt as a reality within your heart, it can be achieved if the discipline and focus is had to pursue what is sought. So the key to conscious creation and living is this: When in quiet contemplation and connected to the higher selves, always remember to paint the picture in vivid detail and true feeling of the thing you do desire, and do not waver or falter from your goal, and eventually it shall come to you through the aid of the Holy Spirit.

The Law of Assumption is a basic law of the universe that can be utilized to obtain the goals we seek. It is a corollary and extension of the principle of the imagination. The Law of Assumption states that we will become and realize what we assume ourselves to already be. However, this does require some explanation. It is not the same as assuming the situation is already presently manifested, for this would lead to bizarre actions and contradictory expression of consensual reality were every person to walk about acting and talking and proceeding as though he were within a reality which was out of synch with all of those around him.

The Law of Assumption is this. Place yourself in the conscious, feeling state where it is assumed and known and understood that that which you seek is already agreed to as an element and part of manifested physical reality and that it is moving through the planes and process of manifestation toward you, that you may soon step into and find yourself living in that place where you desire to be, and thus by living always in the state of assumed expectation of imminent fulfillment, you polarize and energize the energetic bodies to create a resonance that attracts and opens you to those things you have desired and created in your imagination and through the imaginative techniques. And in this way are dreams and wishes realized in an efficient and expeditious manner.

To use this technique to attain and prioritize goals such that all things are achieved with the blessing of Spirit and in accordance with Divine Law and karmically neutral action, this is the way to proceed.

1. When in quiet contemplation, see the image and scenario and situation of the thing or person or action that you desire to be realized, however, from within the detached state.

2. Then in your imagination, while seeing the whole picture, envelop it in the blue light of the Living Sehaji Master, and speak these words with the Inner voice, "I turn my desires over to the Holy Spirit for fulfillment." And in this way shall your heart be known, and the Holy Spirit shall begin to work with you to bring what you wish, but in a way that is balanced and karmically neutral and serves the highest spiritual unfoldment of all

concerned; for remember, the mark of true mastery and the highest level of achievement is not the ability to instantly manifest the things of your desires, but to manifest them in an order and progression and manner that is in harmony with all about you and supports of all life and the development and unfoldment of fellow man and the plans of the Holy Spirit and Sugmad.

3. And so, there can sometimes be a delay in the fulfillment of your desires, but this is just the Holy Spirit working on your behalf to have all balance kept and all karma neutrally positioned so your wishes may be had, but not with a price that should cause you necessary return to the physical or lower plane to repay a karmic debt.

~Sri Leytor

Past Lives

♥ Tap into a past life as an artist using the Law of Three
♥ Learn to trust

How the participant can tap into an artistic talent of the past in one or more of their lifetimes

Be still and know that you are a vital and important part of the God Power. Here is a spiritual exercise to tap into what you have developed in previous lifetimes. Use the Law of Three in ways you will be shown in this spiritual exercise. In each of the three phases, ask permission to work with and then focus in each moment on, an Inner master (whether the Living Sehaji Master, Sugmad, myself, or another Sehaji Master familiar with the arts).

1. Go within your heart consciousness by singing the mantra "**HU-EA-MI-TAY**" 9 times in a rhythmic wave pattern. In conversation with the Master who speaks to your heart, imagine going to the Temple of Golden Wisdom on the Causal Plane as directed. You may meet with Shamus-I-Tabriz also. Ask to be shown and retrieve the fully loaded artistic engrams that carry the artistic talent you wish to develop.

2. Fully and completely trust yourself and the Inner Master. If you cannot do this, do the spiritual exercise *Seeing and Removing Roadblocks to Spiritual Progress* (later in this chapter) for at least three times until you feel comfortable and able to complete this step.

3. With heart open, begin practicing the artistic technique you developed in a former lifetime.

4. Tap into and keep a rhythmic motion. Trust. Know it may take time to fully realize and develop, but start anyway.

5. Look to the Inner in contemplation and dreams for hints and inklings on how to retrieve this information and use it.

6. You may also go to Ekere Tere or another Temple in addition to the one on the Causal Plane. Trust and Flow.

This exercise requires consciousness of the heart, trust and action. If any one ingredient is missing, the resultant art form will lose its effectiveness to inspire and impart truth.

~Master Agnotti

Extend Your Longevity

A contemplative exercise with a mantra that extends longevity and life understanding

1. Ask for life extension and greater understanding.

2. Write your concern or question (one at a time would be less confusing) on the top of a blank page and again, ask the Inner Master for guidance.

3. Sing, *"Heal my heart, my God!"* three to six times.

4. Ask your mind to do research on the topic. You can envision going to a Golden or Blue Library of

Light upon the Earth or Inner Worlds. Let go of all worries or concerns.

5. When awake, you may randomly search the Internet, library, or other written, audio, or video material for answers. Let soul, heart, and your intuitive senses guide you and let answers pop out like popcorn that need to be jotted down.

6. Be sure to keep notes, because what seems obvious and unimportant in one moment could become an important connecting thread that might otherwise be lost.

7. Ask your mind for the results of its research upon its return; write what comes to you and contemplate on it. If you truly do this from soul consciousness in willing alignment with God, there is no limit to what you may discover.

~Dan Rin

Mantras

How to use mantras to obtain guidance during contemplations and throughout the waking hours

Any rhythmic and harmonic pulse that can cause in the heart a desire to be closer to the Light and Sound can be called a mantra. The use of such a word or sound is the

*doorway in your contemplation that allows Soul to be
released from the present situation that the lower bodies
may be engaged in so that it may move unencumbered
through the higher realms of being.*

1. In your morning contemplation, you seek to
   understand what is to be a part of your mission
   each day to spread the Love of Sugmad and to
   bring it forward in your consciousness to be used
   during the course of the day.

2. The use of "**HU**" or your Sacred Word spoken
   inwardly will bring the vibration to the encounter
   that you have been led to as part of your daily,
   karmic duty as a carrier of the Light and Sound in
   The Way of Truth and releases the Love of
   Sugmad into the exchange taking place.

~Master Rebazar Tarz

Develop Prophesy

**A contemplative technique that will develop the
intuitive senses of prophesy**

*The gift of prophecy is for helping yourself learn and grow,
for protection and guidance, but not to wield your will or
invade another person's privacy. To know the probable
future can be a gift or a burden, especially if it contains
harsh realities.*

1. Clear the Inner screen of your mind. Send any negative thoughts or feelings packing on an adventure of their own for the time being or surrender them forever in the River of God. Tune into Sugmad's mainline of love in any way you are already familiar and comfortable. Focus your attention as soul. Sing "*O-PEN-SET.*"

2. Meet with a Sehaji Master. Experiment as some masters know more than others. You may call upon me, if you wish. Greet this spiritual being with the highest respect, ask for guidance, and be totally open and receptive to what comes next.

3. Prophecy classes are taught in a school in the city of Arhirit on the Etheric Plane and in Ekere Tere. Ask your Inner guide to escort you and stay with you to help you learn all you can. Pay attention to details. Write down what you learn as soon as you return to your physical body. Pay attention to messages in your dreams.

Prophecy is not a gift to be taken lightly. It comes with great responsibility. What you learn in Soul Records is only for yourself, unless the Living Sehaji Master gives very strong guidance to tell another person. If in doubt, send a letter to the Living Sehaji Master and contemplate the full situation. If you misuse this gift, it will disappear and may backfire in unwelcome ways. You may use prophecy to understand and prepare for future events, but not change them. Prophecy is a gift only the pure of heart and trustworthy soul need apply for since the responsibility is so great. If it is in alignment with your Soul Contract and your stage of spiritual development, you may have some success. One must be very discreet, emotionally detached, and balanced in all Inner bodies to be able to excel at this highest of arts.

~Master Lemlet

Seeing and Removing Roadblocks to Spiritual Progress

A contemplative exercise that will key our hearts to the solution of a specific roadblock

Roadblocks in life serve specific purposes, even if the lower bodies do not want them to be there. There were good reasons for their creation in the first place and more good reasons for them to remain. However, what once served in a useful way does not always continue to be of benefit. Once you have understood the lessons and wisdom needed, and sincerely wish to remove longstanding roadblocks that you have been unable to remove in any other way, here is a technique that will help.

Warning: Take your time. Be willing to face your emotions and trust whatever comes up for you. It is perfectly fine to get up and move within a session, take as many sessions as needed, and take care of yourself in and between sessions, while you delve deeply into your psyche and Akashic Records for hidden answers. Take as many days or weeks as you need to thoroughly purify all within you that keeps your roadblock in place.

1. Declare your loving devotion to your cause and your intent to carry out your mission, as well as to being in alignment with Sugmad and Its wishes. Do all in the name of Sugmad.

2. Define the specific roadblock you want removed. Keep it simple. You must write it down.

3. Ask Sugmad, Dan Rin, and/or another Master of your choice to show you why you have, and choose to keep, that roadblock in place. After receiving as much insight as you can, ask: "**What else? Please show me a deeper reason.**" Repeat this question two to five more times, for deeper layers of the true reasons "why". Write down all your answers; summarize emerging themes.

4. With Sugmad, Dan Rin, and/or another Master of your choice, take your answers into your heart. Sing your secret word six times, asking for guidance. Contemplate your answers and decide if you still want the roadblock completely removed or altered in some way, remembering that without this roadblock in place, you will have to handle what it has protected you from.

5. In a safe and sacred space within your heart, call forth and meet individually with all souls who are or were involved in creating and sustaining your roadblock, including all aspects of your own self. Discuss what needs to be cleared away. Be as honest, open, and real as possible with your communication; then listen with an open heart to the other side of the story. Embrace what you have heard as truth from the other and give it to Dan Rin. When you have completely forgiven all transgressions and can lovingly hold all persons and souls concerned with Unconditional Divine Love, you will be free of the need for your roadblock. Do not rush through this part of the exercise.

6. Redefine your roadblock and how you wish to reconstruct it to best serve your mission. Ask your chosen guide above to meet with the Lords of Karma to redefine this aspect of your Life Contract. As above, contemplate and write down your experience.

~Sri Leytor

Using Silence to Heighten Intuition

A spiritual exercise that will heighten the use of intuition during focused periods of silence:

1. As always, declare your intentions to God to be Its vehicle for loving service into all the worlds in which you live and move and have your being.

2. Invite the Inner Master to guide and protect you.

3. In silence for 30-60 minutes, settle into your heart and/or Third Eye, and sing three rounds of "*HU-SHHHH-ALL-ONE-SHHH*" three times.

4. Imagine, open to, and feel the higher energies of God coming into you in great and joyful measure. Receive with an open heart and rejoice in the riches of heaven!

5. Tap into this reservoir at any time.

~Dan Rin

Spiritual Comfort

Soul's Development - Now!

♥ Open your heart freely

♥ Determine your next step

A contemplative exercise to give God seekers facilitated development in the area of their needs in life

1. To determine what you really need at this point in your soul development, get on an imaginary beautiful sailing ship and stand at the helm. It might be like the one that took Peter Pan to Neverland. This ship contains no pirates, only angels, spiritual masters, and other souls like you, all loving and focused on achieving and maintaining Sugmad- Absorption, in order to help others.

2. Ask for what you need.

3. Steer your ship toward the destination you intuit as the course needed in this moment.

4. Take turns with the master at the helm.

5. Open your loving heart as you unfurl the ship's sails and soar high above distant lands and oceans.

6. As you sail the high seas, sing: "**HI-DE-HU-JA-VU**," moderately and repeatedly. Laughter is the wind in your sails.

7. Feel the salty spray with the scent of roses.

8. Notice details.

9. Be sure to write down your experience and the answer to what you need upon your return.

~Dan Rin

Universal Soul Movement

♥ Prepare for Universal Soul Movement

♥ Purity of consciousness

How these spiritual keys prepare the God seeker for Universal Soul Movement (USM)

There can be no substantial forward Soul Movement unless there is absolute purity of consciousness. One way to develop this level of purity is through the constant and focused application of acts of love, service, surrender, faith and honor. There are no shortcuts on the road to spiritual freedom; a lazy man will not see the Face of God. However, this is not like a Dickensian sentence of steel gray servitude and mirthless study. There is great joy in all the virtues that the Sugmad has bestowed upon soul; and the greatest joy is in living those virtues and sharing the fruits of that life experience with others. Soul Movement is all about life and giving. There is nothing static in the mercy of God's love for soul; it is always in a state of flux and movement. The endless pool of love within and without soul is always seeking more of Itself. There is no great secret to USM; it is all about staying in the flow of the love and wisdom from your own heart. The spiritual exercises as taught by Dan Rin will facilitate your own natural ability to swim in the Sea of Love and Mercy with a direction and purpose that you as soul were endowed with by the One who awaits your return to the golden fields of Pure Beingness. Words cannot fully express all I have to say on this subject, but I hope to have left you with the "feeling" of the truth in these humble sentences, for I am your humble servant, invited here at the graceful invitation of the Living Master to shed a ray of light and hope for all who travel the roads to spiritual emancipation. Your sincere desire to seek God, light, truth, love, joy and wisdom is your real and first key to unlocking the mysteries within your own heart, spirit, and destiny. This is the launching pad of USM.

~Sri Leytor

♥ Visit the City of Ekere Tere and beyond

♥ The Law of Detachment

This effect is carried to all realms and brings greater stability to the infusion of the Light and Sound in this universe and to this planet as this great healing

of the karmic past takes place through the city of
Ekere Tere.

To be able to do Universal Soul Movement to, within,
and beyond Ekere Tere, try this exercise:

1. Sing "*HU*" or your favorite secret word.

2. Connect to the heart of the current Sehaji Master,
   Dan Rin, or your personal Master who is part of
   the Spiritual Hierarchy, or the Sugmad.

3. Open your heart consciousness, Third Eye, and
   soul consciousness without judgment, and with
   detachment from position or thought, but
   immersed in full beingness.

4. Open to wherever you are. Sense the presence of
   the Spiritual Hierarchy.

5. Look and move just a little. Go with whatever
   comes to you.

6. Practice goodwill toward all teachers throughout
   your day, even the clouds that rain on you, and
   the neighbors who spoil or covet.

7. The Law of Detachment teaches Soul to use every
   lesson in life to see the spiritual heart of all life.
   Milk your experiences for every drop of truth,
   and drink the nectar of the Gods. Practice peace

on earth, goodwill toward all, and you shall usher in the Theater of Today to present the Production of the Light and Sound of Sugmad of the Next Moment. We build the play of life together.

8. Embrace and enjoy every iota of every moment, every sensation and every feeling. Flee not in fear, but stay and be in a detached, neutral, fully aware state, to witness the transformation of the mundane into the Living Divine. Total immersion and sensual delight, coupled with use of the spiritual laws, will enable the chains of the lower bodies and engrammatic signatures to loosen their locks, and let Soul decide what to do next. Balanced detachment and stillness in enough moments of acceptance makes movement into the higher realms a mere shift in consciousness. It is simple, sweet, gentle, and instantaneous as the blink of an eye, or the flutter of a butterfly's wing.

Be here now, always. You stand on the threshold of eternity at any moment you choose. Enjoy!

~Sri Kadmon

♥ Understanding Universal Soul Movement and its practices

As a student in The Way of Truth, the Path to God-Realization, you will pass through realms of consciousness as you approach your true self in Soul. The Astral, Causal, Mental and Etheric Planes are passed through as your initiations take you closer to the Love of Sugmad. Each of these realms carries its own characteristics in awareness in the Inner journey that you will experience, and at each one you will gain valuable lessons on the Inner, as well as the Outer, to strengthen you for the steps into the God Worlds. There are other universes that can be seen and other types of life that will be encountered as you travel these realms above the Etheric. The vehicle that is given to you is your true self as Soul to examine these wonders and to learn more of all aspects of being in the Heart of Sugmad's love. Once you have stepped into this level of beingness, that of Soul, the transition to gaining more understanding takes on a new methodology, that of Universal Soul Movement.

Universal Soul Movement, unlike the idea of astral travel that you may have experienced in lower levels of consciousness, is not connected to the response felt in the causal, which is how the astral adventures are shared within the Lower Worlds. Universal Soul Movement offers the ability to retrieve information from beings of other realms and to transport that information back to this realm where it is translated into useful information, for the vastness of Sugmad's knowledge goes far beyond the confines of this universe as we know it as Soul and reaches into many other aspects of being. Moving toward God-Realization requires a complete change of the vibratory structure of your being to receive complete access to the full benefits of the Light and Sound as the conduit of Sugmad's love to all that exists in this moment. The vehicle of Soul can carry within its heart the information necessary to change the karmic balance laid out by your Soul Contract. It prepares you for the great mission of Soul as it rises to the God Consciousness level and assumes its karmic duties in the changing karma of this time in this Sugmad. What is needed of you is to continue in your contemplation practices to gain the abilities necessary to understand the vast awareness that will be needed as you travel the Inner realms moving toward your Godhood.

~Master Tremulin

♥ Using Universal Soul Movement to Time Travel

Moving on the time track

The use of Universal Soul Movement to move forward and backward upon the time track and view and see events and potential circumstances is a gift to Soul to better aid it in its journeys and unfoldment. The future of a Soul is a set of probable possibilities according to the Life Contract of the Soul and what has been agreed to and is necessary. Some events must be experienced, either sooner or later. Some may be avoided. Some have already been experienced and are not to be experienced again. There is an element of choice involved in the timing of the experience, for Soul does always have free will, and some things may be delayed or accelerated according to the desires and wishes of the one who does have to face them, for not all experiences are of a negative nature, and some are very pleasurable and enjoyable to have. And so, Universal Soul Movement is a way to gain perspective and detachment from the events that lie ahead and to have a measure of self-determination and planning, as to what is to be experienced and when, that the Soul's unfoldment and progression might occur at a pace that is comfortable and desirable.

~Sri Leytor

Spiritual Comfort

Chapter Ten

Working with Karma

Spiritual Comfort

Accepting Higher Spiritual Duties

Consulting with your Oversoul for gaining understanding of higher spiritual duties

When Soul awakens and begins to take responsibility for itself, it can be given higher spiritual duties. This decision is made by the Living Sehaji Master who cooperates with Milarepa and the Grand Council as to Soul's assignment and development of its present spiritual skills. This type of Soul assignment is unique and further reviewed by the Silent Nine. This type of dharma is rarely given by the Living Sehaji Master and is an acknowledgment of the Soul's humility and commitment to Best-Laid Plans.

So when you do seek through contemplation to resolve of a situation or event through the use of Inner means, you must first consult and obtain the permission of the Oversoul who does watch over any other with which you do seek to affect. The exception to this rule is when you do bring the other Soul into the light of the Living Sehaji Master, for then it is the responsibility of the Holy Spirit to manage the situation and the other hierarchies involved and they will understand and any transgressions shall be forgiven. But in any other case, the Oversoul must first be consulted and its permission granted for any action taken, which may affect the other or the circle of its reality or place. For this is why many psychics do often find themselves in peril, for they have violated the agreements and situations put in place by those above, without first consulting or asking permission of the ones that they do serve. And so, each student should not make the mistake of merely seeing physical occurrences as phenomena of only this plane, but should peer behind the curtain to see what does remain hidden and does guide with unseen hands.

To speak to, or obtain permission from, one who does watch over another, you can:

1. In contemplation see the one you know and then behind his head, as if floating on a tether, you may see the one that is known as the Oversoul. And to this one, you must ask your questions and request what you seek to do.

2. If you do not see any cord or another attached, then you must place the one you are seeking within the blue light of the Living Sehaji Master's love, and say to that Soul, *"I do not seek to interfere with the plans of any other. I offer the love of the Living Sehaji Master as proof of my good intention and wish only to send love."*

3. And in this way shall any error be corrected automatically and the student shall be protected from the harm of his ignorance or inability.

~Master Agnotti

Spiritual Comfort

Your Heart

- ♥ Open your heart to greater understanding
- ♥ Release fear and discover wisdom
- ♥ Reveal your Life Contract

A contemplative exercise that will open God seekers hearts to a greater understanding of their lives

1. In a quiet place away from distractions for at least half an hour, relax deeply, let go of all fears and concerns, and then call upon the Inner Master, a beloved spiritual guide, and/or Sugmad for guidance.

2. Imagine a rich, blue veil lifted from your heart and removed from your Third Eye in the center of your head, which awakens all your Inner senses and opens your attention and awareness to a greater understanding of your life.

3. Ask to know your Life Contract.

4. Sing: *"A-LA-TU-SEN-TA"* three times.

5. Listen minutely for the sound of love and joy from the Inner Planes; look for the light of wisdom within. Focus on, surrender to, and feel a radiant love pulsing within the center of your beingness.

6. Record any impressions upon your return. Pay attention to clues in your dreams and Outer World in the next three days and record those, too. The more you practice and know that the answers you seek will come to you, the more you will gain.

~Dan Rin

Prayer for Seekers of the Heart

The way is long and treacherous,

The road well curved and worn.

Yet never shall you find it,

The greatness you have sworn.

For it is so well hidden,

And never shall be revealed.

Unless you truly are given,

The key to move the stone.

I long have journeyed and stumbled,

Along the dusty road.

But never was I given,

The wine to slake my thirst.

Spiritual Comfort

Until I did discern,

The secret that was hidden,

Beneath my very chin.

For the key to certain greatness,

Is not in lines of prose,

Or mental games,

Or clever tricks,

Or power over kingdoms.

It is secreted and hidden,

Beneath the garland rose.

That blooms eternal beauty,

And always does it grow.

Within the heart of champions,

And those who travel home.

And open of their hearts,

To the greatness and are shown.

The secret key to finding,

The sacred Rosetta stone.

That shall guide them in their fortunes,

And never leave them poor,

Or bereft of the love of God.

For the heart is what is given,

To aid all seekers home.

And it must be loved and opened,

If truth is to be won.

For this is the only way,

That God may welcome you home,

And into Its heart above.

~Master Gopal Das

♥ Return to God

Use Your Heart to Return to God

The heart is the only instrument of man capable of realizing the truth of God and the universes below. In my long journey to Mastership, the many lessons I did fail were the ones when I did listen to my mind and not my heart, for the greatest wisdom of man is that which is given from above, and which only may be found in the subtle murmurings and true ways of the heart. I would spend many nights in quiet contemplation, seeking to quiet my fears and the racing of my mind until at last I did begin to achieve of the success which I had sought, and gradually and by degree, the chattering of the mind receded and I did begin to see the truth as it was available and readily laid before me. Then, I did finally know and for myself realize the truth of what had been always said of the heart being the key. As my practice and facility continued, I did begin to see a greater and greater amount of light and love entering into me, until my heart was filled to bursting with the love of the Sugmad, and with my desire to share it with all who would listen to my words or feel of my heart and the truth that I had found.

So, to those who aspire to spiritual greatness, this I do say to you. Return always to your heart, for the wisdom does lie there that shall guide you in your cause, and set you free from pain, and bring you to the very gardens of God-Realization and more, as the heavens do open to you and invite you into their embrace.

The search for spiritual freedom was a long and arduous one, and was not won with power or mental machinations. And so, I did write this poem, that I never would forget the key to seeking of the greatest truth, where it lies hidden beneath.

♥ Share the needs of your heart

A spiritual exercise that will lead you to convey the needs of your heart and emotional expectations

1. After singing *"HU"* five times, you may say the following or rewrite this in your own words: *"Dearest Beloved God, please send a true message of love straight from your heart into mine and into the one I love and wish to know. If this love*

is best for us on all levels of our beingness, please let us know with clearest certainty. I wish to be happy, to give and receive love in equal measure, and to serve in your Best-Laid Plans, Dearest God."

2. Say and feel this with full passion on all levels of your heart, with emotional expectation and intention and sing: *"OU-A-SEN-TA-TU-VAIN"* five times and let your heart speak. Your heart will let you know when to open your eyes and give closure to the exercise.

~Dan Rin

♥ Tuning into Your Potential Partner's Heart

A spiritual exercise that will tune the participant to their potential partner's heart and intention

1. Part I: The first part of this exercise is needed to tune a person to into their own heart. The intention is to know and love their own self, to be in tune with their own heart and desires. This should be done first and foremost before attempting this exercise. For some, this first part may involve a retreat from romantic or sexual relationships, for a time, to reorient to their Inner reality, soul awareness, and Life Contract.

2. Part II: Once this is accomplished to soul's satisfaction, proceed to **tune into the frequency of love in which you wish to live your life**:

   a. Ask Sugmad and the Inner Master to attune you to the correct frequencies of love in alignment with your mission in this life. (This contemplation generally lasts a minimum of twenty minutes.)

   b. In the silence of your heart ask a potential partner on the Inner Planes what their intention is with you and what their heart's true desire is.

   c. Get to know the person on the Inner as well as on the Physical Plane.

   d. Ask the Inner Master to accompany you repeatedly to the Inner sanctum where the two of you can meet and converse, with and without **words, to ascertain your true vibration and** intentions.

   e. Ask to be shown clearly and without resistance how to proceed in outward movement toward building or letting go of the relationship.

   f. At any time in contemplation or when in the physical presence of the person, you may sing silently "*SAY-TU-SEE-TA-SHANTI*" five times. Ask the Oversoul of the person "Are you here to pay a debt, collect a debt, or give and receive mutual love and support for our entire lifetime together?"

g. Keep your heart open to the answer and trust in the wisdom and freedom you will receive.

~Dan Rin

Karma

♥ Clearing karma

♥ Create your life as desired

Contemplation or the stillness of the mind is the technique used by participants in The Way of Truth and others to open the heart connection to the higher self and through non-action, bring the power, wisdom and truth of higher realms into the Physical Plane. This does polarize the lower bodies and reality of the seeker, as has been said before, to effortlessly create the reality that is in accordance and agreement with the Life Contract of each Soul. The spiritual goals of each student are laid out before the shell is taken, by agreement designed and approved with the Lords of Karma to aid the seeker on the path. In the case of participants in The Way of Truth, there has been an agreement made to accelerate this process and quickly burn all karma off, that self-mastery and realization might be achieved and the student might then become the artist and master of all he does encounter.

In the first half of this process, the contemplative action does clear the energetic fields of the seeker and quickly draws to him the karmic patterns and conditions he does need to quickly pay his debts, and the stillness of his heart opens the doorway to higher wisdom and the expression of the divine will and plan. So, the Life Contract is activated and observed and the seeker finds himself in a variety of situations that bring to him the chances and opportunities to resolve the various things that must be done to finally quit the Wheel of 84. For the seeker who is still in the phase of paying back his debts, this is the purpose and power of contemplation.

Once the seeker has repaid all past life and seed karma, then only daily karma remains, and it is a simple thing to repay and settle this in daily life and living. For the Soul at this stage, contemplation does begin to take a new meaning and purpose and function, for the one who has fulfilled the conditions of his life karma and contract now does have the opportunity to begin to create the life that is desired through the spiritual tools of Spirit and techniques of manifestation. As long as what is sought is not directly in violation with any previous agreements or prohibitions, the Soul is free to do as it does please, as long as the balanced state is maintained and adhered to. For those at this stage, contemplation is the way that the higher self is contacted and the powers there are reached and accessed to create what is desired, as long as it is in harmony with Spirit and is done in a way that serves the highest good for all involved, for one cannot simply wish for riches and a life of ease just because all past debts have been paid. These are things that easily can be had and won, but must be done in a way of service to the Holy Spirit and other Souls and in support of Best-Laid Plans of the Sugmad and other hierarchies.

~Master Peddar Zasqz

♥ Karmic Loops

Herein follows a contemplative exercise with a mantra for energetically collapsing the effects of re-occurring karmic loops

1. Imagine you are sitting within a pool of swirling, silver and pink light. It feels like a warm, caressing liquid, but is actually made up of dancing particles of light that sparkle with life and intelligence.

2. Imagine the challenges and karmic loops within your consciousness as ropes around your physical body and allow the swirling waters to loosen and dissolve those ropes, one by one. See them actually break and drop from your body and disappear forever into the shining, silvery pink, living vortex of energy that surrounds and supports you.

3. As you watch the ropes disappear, say this mantra: *"VO-LE-TU-SA-MANA-TE"* (pronounced "voh lay too sah mahnah tay") three times.

4. Do this exercise every day for five days. Thereafter, do it whenever you feel the need for reinforcement or simply for relaxation and rejuvenation. Blessed be to all followers of the Light and Sound of God.

~Dan Rin

Giving Unconditional Love to All

To give unconditional love to all and practice this position and technique, the following exercise may be followed to facilitate the way.

1. Upon rising each morning, and while bathing or contemplating, the student may repeat five *"HU's"* and then to the Master say *"I wish to be a perfect vehicle for light for all I encounter today."*

2. And in this way shall the bodies be polarized to exemplify this state and give and show the love that is desired to be in the proper place.

The second way is:

When you meet another Soul each day, imagine the heart each time unfolding, like a rose in perfect bloom, and the light of God outpouring to reach the one you meet and stand with in friendship or whatever other circumstance.

And in these ways will you become accustomed and truly begin to train your heart to be open and giving of the detached goodwill and compassion that is the key and way.

~Sri Leytor

Filtering Out Negativity in the Mind

A contemplative technique that filters out negativity embedded in the mind

An exercise was given to discover the negative engrams that interrupt the progress of the participant who seeks to move toward the God Worlds. This mantra is a shorter form that is specifically tuned for the mind's negativity. This is best used when a negative thought occurs during your day that must be removed : *"NUM-SAT-HA-YATA."*

Spiritual Comfort

If used in the morning contemplation, this mantra can be set in place to activate when the heart senses the mind sliding toward negative thoughts.

~Babaji

Prayer for Facing Trials

A prayer for daily living and facing life's trials

Read this prayer out loud and sing five "*HUs*" thereafter and begin your day.

"Come into my heart, my Lord,

I pray to you each day.

Show me how to live my life

While walking in Your Way.

Help me to be willing

To do all that you may ask.

Guide me to Your Heart Within

From there I do each task.

Protect me from the dangers

Lying in my mind and out.

Show me how to surrender

All my fears and doubts.

Lead me to let go

Of things that are not mine.

And live forever in your joy

I will be forever Thine. "

~Master Prisca

True Success

The heart and love's true success

Love's true success is founded on facing the other with the intention of serving them and their highest spiritual good and truth. This is not to say that one must become subservient to the other, for this is not the case. What it does mean is to always follow the truth of our own heart with honesty and truth and respect for the wishes of the other. None may be bound against their will and yet be free within their hearts. It is not the swiftest way to wisdom to ignore the voice of your own heart or to bind another against their wishes or desires or the truth they have found for themselves or wish to seek or explore. When one is seeking to create a relationship of love and service, this is the constant test. This is a very powerful postulate to use to begin your day.

1. Always check and ask your self by going into contemplation by just saying **"Sugmad lead me in**

serving my loved one in the highest aspects of love, respect and freedom."

2. Then sing five *"HUs"* and open your eyes gently.

~Dan Rin

Chapter Eleven

Visiting Spiritual Cities and Special Classes

Spiritual Comfort

Agam Des

Here follows a spiritual exercise that will allow the God seeker a glimpse or a chance to walk the streets of Agam Des

1. Imagine you are on a tiger hunt. You are walking through a jungle of lush green plants and colorful flowers. You are seeking the great Bengal Tiger who wears a crown of rubies and emeralds. There are many tigers roaming the jungle, but only one who wears the crown.

2. Seek him out; he will come to you when you say this mantra three times: *"DOMINAY-PLATU-AGAM-DES."*

3. Now he appears and you can approach this majestic beast without fear. He bows and allows you to climb upon his back. You ride with him through the maze of the jungle that gets deeper and more difficult to navigate. At times you can barely see through the tangle of wild undergrowth, trees and foliage. But soon there comes a clearing and a white stone door becomes visible through a soft, golden mist. Here the tiger leaves you.

4. Approach the door and say this mantra three times: *"MANATAY-SI-PLATU-AGAM-DES."*

5. Now the door begins to open very slowly, so slowly that you must strain to see what lies beyond. **Now sing "HU" five times and then sing "Dan Rin" five times.** Keep looking. If your heart is open and filled with love, you may be allowed to catch a glimpse or even walk the streets of this magnificent and forbidden city.

6. Stay in this contemplation for at least fifteen minutes.

7. If nothing comes, try again for the next six days.

May you be blessed by all that is Holy.

~Master Milarepa

Astral, Causal, and Mental Worlds

A contemplative exercise that will give the God seeker a glimpse of the Astral, Causal, and Mental Worlds

In the ship and exercise above, you can set your course for each successive plane, from the Physical upward to Sugmad.

1. Set your dial with awareness of the Physical Plane to "1." Feel as fully as you please all sensations

you can in your Physical Body. Sing "***HU-NA-TRE-NA-SET.***"

2. After you tire of the Physical Plane, set your dial to "2"; place "2" in your Middle Eye and feel with Astral senses the parameters of the Astral Plane as you leave the Physical Plane behind.

3. Continue to set your dial higher one increment at time, from number "3" through "9" or higher. Continue as long as you can and increase this exploration, shortening the time you spend in the lower realms, as you lose interest in them and desire to explore the higher.

4. You are in control. You can set your dial and set your own course. Do so in alignment with Sugmad and Its open and welcoming loving heart, which is at this minute calling to you. There is no limit to the heights to which you can travel in full consciousness.

5. Be diligent and patient with yourself and enjoy!

~Dan Rin

Ekere Tere, City of Light

A contemplative exercise that will develop in the God seeker a greater understanding of the universal laws

Decide what you would like to learn about the universal laws and The Way of Truth and how much time you are willing to commit to this endeavor. Regularity and rhythm in your daily schedule is important. With sincerest devotion daily for at least a week, do the following:

1. Upon arising and upon retiring for the night, say silently to God in your breast: *"I let go of all my fears and open fully and completely to the full and pure Love, Grace, and Wisdom of Eternal Sugmad, right here, right now."* Begin to say this prayer every hour, then more often as you remember to do so. The more you say it, the more you will respond.

2. Upon retiring at night or in contemplation, set your intention to have Universal Soul Movement in full consciousness to the golden city of Ekere Tere. You are invited to attend my classes or any other for which you are able. Sing your secret word and ask the Living Sehaji Master for assistance and guidance. Trust what comes into your awareness, whether it looks like what you

expected or not. Unless it is clearly harmful, go with it.

3. Envision standing before the gates in the corner of the high golden wall surrounding the city. Ask Sri Treylen, the guardian, for entry and to attend the class of your choice. He will ask you a question. Tune into what he is asking and answer most sincerely from your heart.

4. Always singing your secret word, and letting it evolve as it may, pay attention to minute details of form, color, vibration, feeling, message, etc. Tune in. You are an intricate part of the fabric of the city now. Be careful of the trace you leave behind.

5. Once you gain entry into Ekere Tere, walk slowly down the tree lined corridors. Again pay minute attention to sights, sounds, smells, tactile sensations, your thoughts, and other occurrences within you and around you.

6. Travel to a class and take a seat. Tune in to the Inner Master or the Sehaji Master giving his or her gifts. Participate in the lecture as instructed. In my classes, we will often take "field trips" deeper into the Inner Worlds. Go with the experience as long as you can.

7. You may leave the way you came, take the K bridge out, watch events in the center of the city,

or do whatever you are compelled or invited to do. Most importantly - Enjoy! I give you Blessings of beauty and wisdom. This is a treat beyond any available before. Once you learn how to do this, you might decide to visit Ekere Tere more frequently and regularly. You may visit once per week or month and help develop the group consciousness that will form the heart of the leadership of your planet into the future.

~Master Parmenides

Gabriel's Classes

A contemplative exercise that will enable the participant the opportunity of sitting in one of my spiritual classes in Ekere Tere, City of Light

This technique is given as my gift to you. As always, what you do is your choice.

1. In quiet contemplation, after softly or silently singing your secret word or "**HU**," call to me to invite me to meet with you in your favorite sacred place on the Inner Planes. Imagine me directly in front of you. I hold you in the most sacred space of love and affection.

2. I invite you to hold both of my hands to make direct contact. Feel the love and joy I feel for you.

Feel our hearts connect. Feel warm loving light enter into your heart and fill your entire being with a pure love for God Almighty, known by whatever name you prefer. Look deeply into my eyes. My eyes are pure sky blue, reflecting the vast open territory of Sugmad's creation. My hair and all that comes forth in manifestation from me is pure gold. The light radiating from me is purest white, the result of eons of unconditional surrender to the ways, will, and love for the Greatest One.

3. Trust in me, for I shall not lead you astray. Come with me to stand outside the entrance into Ekere Tere. Let us call to Sri Treylen, the guardian, to open the gates and allow your entry. Talk with him about any concerns and also get directions to the current class you wish to take. In the future, when you have mastered this technique, you may return here without me and proceed as described.

4. Sing the mantra: *"GA-BREE-EL-SOOG-MAD-AUM."*

5. Enter the main gate and walk with me to the destination described by Sri Treylen. Notice as many details of buildings, landscaping, other souls, smells, sights, sounds, and feelings you have along the way. Pay very close attention to your feelings, thoughts, intuition, and interactions

with other beings and with me. Above all, stay in your loving heart as it opens completely to the surroundings, and joyfully and playfully receive what comes your way. I invite you to dance and move in ways you might not dare or be able to do in your physical surroundings. Fear is not allowed within the gates; a bearer of fear will be expelled immediately. You are safe here, should you be allowed entry. All are screened very carefully and must be of pure heart and intent to enter the city walls.

6. When you enter the room where I will be teaching, find your place and wait for my position in the center of the room. You may greet beloved friends. Focus on what I convey, participate when invited, and make a postulate to remember what you can.

7. Please write down details of your experience in a special journal upon your return to waking life. My teachings, and that of other Masters from this temple, will be imparted to you in methods beyond your mind's ability to comprehend. Symbols, messages, and further intuitions will continue to appear in your consciousness for a time to come. Return daily for full measure and ability to appreciate what wisdom and experiences you have been imparted. This is, indeed, a sacred gift and invitation which has never been presented in this way in the full history of sentient beings in

the physical realm. Welcome to my home, and Ekere Tere. Blessed be.

~Archangel Gabriel

Mental Plane

♥ **Focusing thoughts on purity and love**

A technique to facilitate a higher level of thought activity and purity is this:

1. **Throughout** the day or during contemplation imagine of yourself upon the Mental Plane. And there imagine all your thoughts as balloons that are filled with air and floating all about you.

2. Now, as you do wish to increase the activity and purity of your thoughts, imagine all the balloons as they begin to rise and are filled with golden light and sparkling diamonds that float within the air.

3. And as these thought balloons do begin to fill and rise, they do collect in the highest possible region within the Mental Plane where it does meet the Etheric and Soul Planes.

4. And as the final measure, imagine long cords of gold and silver attaching these balloons to your body on that plane.

5. And in this way, with persistence and discipline and gentle training, shall the Mental Body learn and always focus its thoughts and activity on the purity of love and higher ideals in its workings through each day, and this shall aid the seeker and bring him closer to heaven's gates and his home above.

~Sri Leytor

Plato

Plato has opened a vortex for the participants to speak with him about the heart, mind and body as well as secrets of the universe.

1. You can call upon Plato by singing the spiritual name of *"Dan Rin"* five times and then call Plato's name three times.

2. Envision yourself speaking with Plato.

3. Ask him any question you choose and listen to your heart. It does not matter if you do not see his face.

~Dan Rin

Spiritual Comfort

Sat Nam's Court

Here follows a contemplative exercise that will give the God seeker entry and an understanding of what awaits in Sat Nam's Court

1. Imagine you are comfortably riding on a huge elephant; you are securely seated in a chair strapped to the elephant's back and are moving steadily toward a monumental gate with two pillars at either side at the tops of which are torches burning with fire that reach far into the sky. There is the sound of drums coming from beyond the gate that have a rhythmic, soothing beat. They beat with the rhythm of your own heart. As you approach the gates, they begin to slowly swing open and you can begin to see what lies in wait.

2. Pass through the gates and say this mantra three times: "*SULAY-TA-OVAY-TIKA.*"

3. You are now being greeted by two servants in white clothing and white turbans. They help you down from the elephant's back and lead you to an altar that sits in the open space of a massive garden of tropical plants and flowers. There they leave you in silence and solitude.

4. Soon, a light glows from the center of the altar and within this light a face begins to appear, or it may just be two eyes that shine from within the light.

5. Look into the eyes and know that you are communing with a reflection of the great Sat Nam Himself. Simply gaze into the eyes of this holy manifestation of God and allow whatever wisdom, knowledge or information He has for you to enter into you, through your heart. Blessed Be.

~Dan Rin

Sea of Love and Mercy

A contemplative technique with a mantra that will allow the participant the opportunity of viewing the Sea of Love and Mercy

The God seeker may visit and view the great Sea of Love and Mercy by learning to negotiate the subtle distinctive levels of vibrating energetic frequencies emitted in the various levels of God. The seeker must learn how to move from coarser to finer vibrations and learn how to develop great stamina in order to integrate the various levels into his or her consciousness.

1. To begin this integration process and view the great Sea of God, one should sit quietly and

undisturbed for at least 30-60 minutes. Place your attention on the Heart Center.

2. Feel the love God has for you, listen with silent ears to the beating of the heart, and call to the Inner Master.

3. Ask him to come and guide you from the place where you sit, out of the physical body, through the various levels of finer vibration, and into the 14th plane, where dwells the Great Spiritual Ocean.

4. Sing *"Sugmad, bring me home ."*

5. Feel yourself rise slowly and steadily through your physical body, then your emotional body, then your memory banks of the unconscious mind, then the vast clarity of the mental worlds, and finally through the intuitive functioning of the Etheric Plane.

6. You will then cross the barrier to the Soul Plane and then move upward and inward through successively finer levels of beingness. You do not need to know how to do this "properly," and do not wonder if you are doing this right, for to ponder these aspects is to lose any benefit gained from surrendering to this process. Allow the Inner Master to take you. Hold the goal lightly in mind and surrender.

7. Whenever you see the Light of God and hear the beautiful music as it changes in each succeeding plane, keep going. It is important to keep your imagination moving toward a higher love and Light and Sound. Soul will know when you have arrived, but the mind will think that the first plane of brilliant Light and Sound is heaven, the home of God. This is not true. God's true home is far beyond. You must trust that what you get is where you need to be for now.

8. Keep practicing and watch your Inner Worlds expand and your experiences grow in a most loving way. Take the time to do this repeatedly.

~Dan Rin

Shamballa

Herein follows a contemplative exercise to request entry into the divine city of Shamballa and gain training under one of its many spiritual teachers

1. Imagine you are a passenger waiting for a train to take you to Shamballa. You stand before golden railroad tracks that shimmer with a spiritual luminescence. From the far distance you hear the haunting sound of the train whistle like a mantra of peace and solitude. You see the train approaching – a magnificent silver vehicle with

clear, shining windows. It stops in front of you and the door opens for you to enter.

2. Go inside and take a seat by a window. Now it begins to roll toward your destination and the only thing missing is the ticket for entrance. Call the Conductor forth who has your ticket in his possession. Say this mantra three times: "*VO-TE-LA-TU-SHAMBALLA.*"

3. The Conductor appears before you and places the ticket for entry into Shamballa in your open hand. It is white with gold lettering and has your name in the center. That is enough to get you in.

4. Now the train stops at the gates to your divine destination. Walk to the gate and give the Guardian your holy ticket. That is all that is required for entrance into this great spiritual city. A Master will be waiting to escort you and provide whatever training you need at this time. Go with peace and love in your heart!

~Dan Rin

Spiritual Cities Listed in The Way of Truth Eternal – Book I

How one may employ Universal Soul Movement to visit the spiritual cities described in *The Way of Truth - Book I*

1. When you are rested and have at least one half hour completely undisturbed, sit in a comfortable position.

2. You may play relaxing music or sing any of the sacred words or sounds that have helped you in the past to enter into realms above.

3. Relax and envision your heart wide open as never before.

4. Call to Our Lord Sugmad and, in these or your own words, say: *"Sugmad, I declare myself to be your loving, devoted vehicle for Divine Love now and evermore. Please send me a helper, Dan Rin, another Sehaji Master or angel, to escort me to the city of Ekere Tere, then on to _____ (your desired final destination)."*

5. A significant part of this process of Universal Soul Movement to Ekere Tere is complete surrender. What good does it do to go where you have not consciously gone before and try to remain in full control? The River of Life is wild and free; so, too,

must you be to enter into it. Remember that Sugmad loves you and bolsters you. Let go of control and join with masters of old who have gone where you seek and know of methods they are willing to teach you. Trust is not easy for many souls in the physical realms, but trust is essential to journeying in the Inner realms. So, trust!

6. Stay awake and be receptive to the tiniest of nuances. Allow the mind to rest; or for best results, send the mental body out to work on other tasks while you, Soul, contemplate, as is taught by Dan Rin in other writings. Your trust in the Sugmad, in the Sehaji Masters, and in the process of unfoldment is essential and cannot be emphasized enough.

7. So to summarize:

    a. Set your spiritual, physical, emotional, and mental scene

    b. Declare your intentions and ask for guidance

    c. Relax

    d. Trust

    e. Join with the larger unity of souls who walk in The Way of Truth

f. Enjoy your experience! Repeat, repeat, and repeat!

~Sri Leytor

Sugmad's Heart

To experience the wormhole, a doorway in space, and move instantly into Sugmad's heart

1. Stand in the open vortex of Ekere Tere and feel the eye of the Sehaji align with your heart. Devotion is key.

2. Change your size to fit the city in your body, and then feel it around you many miles long. Change is key.

3. Use the law of 3 – focus on Sugmad (the originator, transmitter of all frequencies of love), the Master (highest of Sugmad's creations), and self/soul (in the individual's highest aspect) as receiver. Awareness is key.

~Sri Kadmon

Spiritual Comfort

Temples of Wisdom

We of the Sehaji order wish to accept you in these Inner Worlds of learning, but one must come with an open heart to gain the understanding of the ancient secrets and wisdom that has been chronicled for eons.

1. To prepare for this journey, sit quietly and focus your mind on the Third Eye in the center of your forehead.

2. Then let your consciousness move to the center of the heart chakra and sing *"HU"* five times slowly.

3. Call to Dan Rin three times very slowly, asking him to help you open your heart to the Light and Sound that will guide you to us.

4. To let your self move to your beingness in Soul, use the word *"SU TALAY."* (SÜ TÄ LÄ) This will generate the vibration to allow you to move with Dan Rin into a deeper experience of Universal Soul Movement and to be introduced to the many Temples of Wisdom and knowingness that, as you gain a deeper awareness of your true selfless heart, entrance will be granted to you.

~Master Rebezar Tarz

Understanding and Implementing Commitment to the Law of Divine Love

Here are some variations on spiritual exercises to explore various aspects of the Law of Divine Love:

1. Feel self as an aggregate of souls moving around Ekere Tere.

2. Feel self as the Sehaji Master, the manifested body of Sugmad, with souls moving through your body as the City of Light.

3. Move love through every cell of your body – with full awareness and unconditional love for all creation and its inter-connection.

These spiritual exercises upgrade the flow of Sugmad's energy, and allow it to flow without fear and impediment, a necessary step to balance and maintenance of that flow. That is why fierce Divine Love of some religious groups is so powerful. They may not have balance and accurate structure of beliefs to go to Sugmad, but their intensity of love and devotion can be vital to creating movement and change in the hearts and minds of all of humankind. Their inaccurate elitist notions of separation may not be in alignment with Sugmad's heart, but are used as fodder for the dark forces to create friction and lessons for Soul's education and entertainment.

Spiritual Comfort

The Way of Truth is gaining momentum on planet Earth now to serve as a wayshower to place the interlocking pieces together again, to complete the circuit so the unconditional love current can again be in place for the full activation, maintenance and balance of Sugmad's love. Like a railroad track when dismembered, only a few pieces need be removed for there to be no flow and no travel along its route. Let none of us who have made our commitment, agreements, and contract with Sugmad become a circuit breaker. We are all needed to completely love Sugmad, love one another, and love ourselves to a higher degree than has ever been possible before this time, in order to usher in an era and renaissance of Divine Love.

~Master Kadmon

Chapter Twelve

Achieving Goals and Dreams

Express via the Arts

Express and purify your self

Inspiring words of wisdom and love to impart to those who aspire to achieve in the arts

Take heart – the arts are as natural as breathing. First and foremost, as the Star Tetrahedron implies, the center of all life is and must be the Heart of Sugmad and the human heart. Sugmad awaits souls to express Its divine love in both esoteric and practical ways in which souls express it on your planet. Most important is your state of consciousness when expressing. It is fine to express in any media about daily events and feelings that are not of the highest realms. As the outward arms of the Star Tetrahedron imply, the life force of Sugmad's love moves out from its center, connects to one another, and points in every direction. Art must relate to the recipient observer and touch him or her in some way, in order to awaken that soul on its life adventures. If the art form can touch Soul and bring it closer to higher realms, so much the better. Much of art expression can and must reach souls and elevate them on some or all levels.

1. Express your heart. Express yourself to be rid of dross and impurities, and teach others that life can and does improve with reflection on higher aspects. Beauty and tenderness can do as much, if not more, than esoteric wisdom of the ages. If the

artist returns to the heart consciousness and creates from there, magic happens.

2. Listen and observe what your art expression does to you. Is this what you wish to put out in the world for others to absorb? Is there some value to you that others would benefit from as well? What does Sugmad and your Inner guidance tell you is right or not right about your piece, and how can you re-work it to impart the purity of its message? The more you stay tuned into the flow of the Holy Spirit, the more your work will convey the vitality of God's message.

~Master Agnotti

Making the Right Choices

How to weigh spiritual wisdom

1. Imagine that you are sitting in a classroom and there is a large blackboard at the front of the room. Whenever there is a choice to make in your daily life, see yourself going to that Inner blackboard and writing down the question of the choice you face.

2. Then take an imaginary eraser and wipe out the question. Close your Inner eyes and say this

mantra: *"VO-LE-TU-SO-MA-TE"* (pronounced "voh lay too soh mah tay.") Say it three times.

3. Then open your eyes and look for the answer to your question. If it is not immediately visible on the blackboard, say, *"Thank you for the wisdom of my choice,"* and go on with your day. The right and wisest choice will thereafter be impressed upon your consciousness and you will simply KNOW what to do. Blessed be to all sincere travelers of the Light and Sound.

~Dan Rin

Increasing Awareness of Knowledge

How to expand and widen awareness of life's gems of knowledge

Within each of your lives there are treasures yet unfound of the great gifts with which you have been blessed. Let me come to you and guide you to these wonders that may still be hidden from your awareness.

1. Sit in quiet contemplation with a focus on the opening of the heart.

2. Say the mantra, *"PARA-TA-HAR-BRAHMAN"* <u>five times</u>. Then call to me, Babaji, <u>three times</u>.

3. When you feel my presence, we shall say this mantra together for 5 to 10 minutes.

4. As the knowledge of these things may be unknown to you, use this technique three days and your Inner vision will be focused on these things that we will find together.

5. What will be revealed to you will happen over the next two weeks after we have spent this time together. You will find them in some place and experience where you least expect to.

~Babaji

Appreciating Literature and Poetry

A contemplative exercise by which participants can develop their own appreciation and writing of poetry and literature

1. Set your intention and/or form a question. Write it down, preferably in a notebook or computer where you will be writing when you come out of contemplation. Have pen and paper or other recording device of your choice always at hand, because you can never know in advance when the Holy Spirit will move through you.

2. Declare yourself to be now and evermore a pure vehicle for the Great Sugmad. Sing *"HU"* or your secret word and meet me in Ekere Tere in my classroom. Listen, observe, open your heart, and follow instruction.

3. Come with me where I shall direct, and partake of the open living Vortex of Universal Love. Feel free to dance, leap, swirl, or move in any way you choose to infuse yourself with and express the Holy Current of God. Pose your question or request and sing the mantra: *"AHH"* in one drawn out breath. Breathe in **HU**. Repeat.

4. Receive the Current of Intense Sound and Light, the Divine Essence of God, pouring forth from the vortex into your open heart, into every orifice, crevice, pore, and cell of your Inner and Outer bodies. Surrender to the Holy Spirit completely with the utmost trust that it will protect and guide your best interests and the best interests for all you come in contact with today, and for the greater society at large. Know with all of our assurances and your own knowingness as Soul that, no matter what you have ever done and whatever shame you carry, you are part and parcel of Its great creation and important to Its mission. You can act more lovingly now.

5. After you return to your waking consciousness, you must write what you experienced, or it will surely be lost, and then follow through with your intention. This step is as important as any other. If you follow through with your intention, you will be signaling the spiritual hierarchy that you are receptive to its guidance. If you do not, you will diminish the current flowing through you and increase the tests you will be given to prove you are serious in your spiritual quest.

6. Enjoy your adventure in reading poetry and the literature of the best minds and loving souls who lived upon your planet. Have fun expressing what you have experienced in writing. Keep your Inner experiences to yourself until months later when you have integrated all you can from it.

7. Enjoy your interactions with others throughout your day. Continue to share your love and the gifts received from the Holy Spirit.

You are the living embodiment of Sugmad, as is every other soul! Know it and act accordingly. Your life is Sugmad's gift to you. What you do with it, and how you express yourself, is your gift in return. How precious it is!

~Master Rumi

Develop the Discipline of Silence

How the God seekers can develop the discipline of silence within themselves

The hardest aspect of silence is learning to hold and not release tension through talking.

1. Move the energy created and felt as tension into physical activity, such as exercise, dance, stretching, martial arts, or other forms that you prefer. Feel the power of the energetic build-up surge through you in a very conscious way, and give this power as a gift back to Sugmad. There is no need to be stingy with what you have been given. Although the whispering of the Holy Spirit has been given for your awareness alone, in many cases you can share the joy and love you have received without words. Gifts of love through deeds carry far more power than words. Remember that words are about one sixth of the message you communicate all the time. The rest of communication is conveyed through your body language and actions.

2. You may also use the energy created in silence to move the nine pointed tetrahedron you have begun to visualize in your Third Eye, or cleanse your chakras, or open your heart to the

Light and Sound, or extend your energy field in the fullness of love, or any other countless spiritual exercises you may do throughout the day. Energy is fuel for movement. Once you experiment and develop techniques that work for you to further align your thoughts, feelings, heart, and soul with the vision and mission of the Sehaji and Sugmad, the sooner you will want to maintain and further enhance your discipline of silence within. You will soon see that the benefits to you and others far outweigh being stuck in old patterns of excessive talk.

3. Again, regularity and repetition can retrain even the most hardened body, heart, and mind. Try using two hours per day, preferably, but not necessarily, only from the hours of nine to ten o'clock each day. Make your discipline a devotion to Sugmad, with your most loving heart wide open.

4. When you find yourself stuck, try something new. Repetition does not mean boring and stagnant; it can mean new and refreshing spiritual exercises and Universal Soul Movement experiences again and again. Change is vital. Play and use your scientific, empirical mind to understand how the process works.

5. If you need to express, do it on paper, on the computer, or other media just for you. Sing what you are learning through sounds without meaning; listen and learn from all life on a vibratory, not verbal, level. These practices help develop a love for silence.

6. Watch your planted seeds grow into fields of fragrant green and you will reap a harvest the likes of which you may never have dreamed possible. Envision your silence falling like rain on parched earth, rejuvenating and replenishing. Use your creative imagination and creative intelligence to the maximum.

7. Have fun with it. Where you may have loved sharing everything with others, know that some harvests are for you alone and can be shared later. You may share with the Inner Master or other Sehaji Masters on the Inner Planes and gain great friendships and connections there.

Nothing can limit you and nothing can harm you, if you but observe the simple and powerful Law of Silence.

~Master Pythagoras

Glossary

A

Astral Plane The Astral Plane, also called the emotional plane, is the powerhouse for physical movement. A more sensitive transformer of the higher energies than the physical body, this plane is also the realm of the emotions.

B

Best-Laid-Plans Sugmad's dream for its creation of the universe and all life forms; a dream in which sleeping souls tested, tried and proven through the fires of purification eventually awaken. Once fully awake, Sugmad's children see each other as brothers and sisters, person to person, nation to nation. Love, peace, harmony and Sugmad's abundance reign.

C

Causal Plane The Causal Plane was created as a storehouse for memory to be accessible for the use of soul in any of the Lower Worlds.

Charity Charity is a gift of love with no strings attached.

Contemplation This is an active form of engaging the mind in activity aligned with soul, and in this way, differs from prayer and meditation.

D

Darshan Is a gift of love from the Godman that fills the recipient's heart with joy, for the face of a living God has been seen.

E

Ego A part of the mind, ego's purpose is survival. Too often seduced by power, in actuality, the ego is like a ping pong ball when compared to the sun.

Etheric Plane The Etheric Plane, sitting just below the Soul Plane, is the highest region of the Mental Plane, and was created to begin soul's descent into the Lower Worlds.

F

Forgiveness Is one of the keys to ascension and spiritual achievement. To truly forgive, one's soul must be filled with compassion.

G

God-Absorption Involves seeing, knowing and being a son or daughter of Sugmad. It is the ultimate reunification with Sugmad such that when you move, Sugmad moves.

God-Realization The cellular recognition, ignited from within, that you are a part of God.

Great Divide This refers to the separation of the heavenly worlds from the Lower Worlds. Below the Great Divide points to the worlds below the Soul Plane; above the Great Divide considers planes inclusive of the Soul Plane and higher.

H

Heart Center The heart center is located around the physical heart, however the term refers to this area as a chakra or a location that acts as a conduit for divine energy.

HU HU is the sacred gift from this Sugmad to the souls of this universe who are ready to receive the heart of its truth. As the final key to the highest plane in the long journey through all the lower realms of this universe back to the heart of God, it can open every door. Use HU to seek the destination of your heart.

I

Initiations Initiations acknowledge souls passing tests on their journeys home to the heart of Sugmad. They provide structure and catapult souls to new uncharted territory in each successive plane of their journeys.

Inner Inner describes the focus on that which is not seen with physical eyes, but exists as experiential phenomena nonetheless.

J *(none)*

K

Kal Niranjan Kal Niranjan was designated by Sugmad as Lord of the Lower Planes. Kal is not malicious or vicious as he has been portrayed. He merely carries out his assigned duties with precision and deft artistry.

Karma Also known as the Law of Cause and Effect, karma is the law by which soul reaps the rewards or experiences of the consequences of prior actions, even from past lives, whether soul remembers them or not.

L

Law of Compassion This Law allows soul a way to give love under any circumstances.

Law of Freedom Freedom creates, contains, and maintains the vital energies of life. This Law enables Sugmad to learn of Its true and full potential.

Law of Noninterference This Law renders respect to all life. This is accord with Sugmad's gift of free will to all souls, and allows souls to evolve in their own unique ways.

Law of Silence Little understood, but greatly needed, silence is pregnant with power. Silence holds great energetic *frequencies of the Light and Sound.*

Law of Unity This Law is a reminder that our true goal and state is union with Sugmad and one another.

Life Contract A Life Contract specifies a mission; it gives direction as an agreement to move in certain areas to gain awareness and expertise unique to self in relation to others to fulfill a greater purpose.

Light and Sound These are the primary emanations from Sugmad that constitute the Life Force, source of all life and All That Is.

Love Love is the essential nature of Sugmad, soul, and all manifestation. Love creates and sustains our universe; the absence of love destroys.

M

Mental Plane The mental realm, or mind without physical brain stuff, was made to take the intuitive impulses and step them down a few notches more. The Mental Plane includes the Etheric, however, the Etheric is of a higher vibratory quality and sits directly below the Soul Plane.

N

Non-power The non-power is the receiver, the receptacle of Sugmad's Power. To experience the non-power, one must achieve true detachment with full loving awareness.

O

Outer Refers to phenomena that can be perceived by the physical senses, as distinct from "Inner."

P

Physical Plane The Physical Plane was created for souls to experience gross and corporeal beauty and pain through sensory apparatus. As the lowest plane, it completes Sugmad's playground and grand experiment for the education and evolution of souls, sparks of Sugmad's own Self, units of Sugmad's awareness.

Q *(none)*

R *(none)*

S

Self-Realization This is the first stage of soul's entrance into the heavenly worlds as it journeys into these worlds of beingness and pure love. Here the aspirant recognizes her or himself as Soul, not as the lower bodies soul uses to gain experiences in the Lower Worlds.

Soul Soul is a part of God, "made in His image" and is actually the same in nature as Sugmad.

Soul Contract In each incarnation, soul enters with an aim or a purpose. As reductive units of God, we each have unfolding to do based on the karma we have created. A Soul Contract is an intelligent agreement that directs a particular soul's growth toward its ultimate destination, reunification with God.

Soul Movement/Universal Soul Movement Soul movement or Universal Soul Movement is a change in consciousness through which soul perceives realities beyond those that exist in this physical realm. Some may experience a movement in their soul body as it travels through the various dimensions; others may simply become aware of a phenomenal experience without any sensation of movement.

Sugmad This constitutes a pure name for God, the Creator of this universe and all life forms.

T

Third Eye Located a little above the space between the eyebrows and about an inch within, the Third Eye is a receptor of Inner visions. The pineal gland is its physical representation.

Temples of Wisdom These are Inner Temples where spiritual training, purification and the imparting of secrets occur. These spiritual temples are contained within vortices of varying degrees that transmit frequencies coming from the highest realms.

U

Universal Laws Sugmad established universal laws to bring order into consciousness from chaos. Like a train track for trains, or the Internet for ideas, universal laws provide a structure for creation and manifestation.

V *(none)*

W

Worlds

The *Higher Worlds* refer to creation starting from and extending beyond the Soul Plane up to the fountainhead of Sugmad or the Sea of Love and Mercy.

The *Lower Worlds* encompass creation just below the Soul Plane, specifically the Etheric Plane and down to this, the Physical Plane. The gap between these two sets of worlds is called the "Great Divide."

X *(none)*

Y *(none)*

Z *(none)*

Index

For more information

you are invited to visit:

www.thewayoftruth.org

Notes

Notes

_____

_____

_____

_____

_____

_____

_____

_____

_____

_____

_____

_____

_____

_____

_____

_____

_____

_____

_____

_____

_____

_____

_____

_____

_____

_____

_____

_____

Notes

_____
_____
_____
_____
_____
_____
_____
_____
_____
_____
_____
_____
_____
_____
_____
_____
_____
_____
_____
_____
_____
_____
_____
_____
_____
_____
_____
_____
_____

Notes

_____
_____
_____
_____
_____
_____
_____
_____
_____
_____
_____
_____
_____
_____
_____
_____
_____
_____
_____
_____
_____
_____
_____
_____
_____
_____
_____
_____
_____

Made in the USA
Charleston, SC
01 May 2012